BOTTLEMANIA

BOTTLEMANIA

How Water Went on Sale and Why We Bought It

Elizabeth Royte

BLOOMSBURY

Published by Bloomsbury USA, New York
Distributed to the trade by Macmillan

All papers used by Bloomsbury USA are natural, recyclable products made from wood grown in well-managed forests. The manufacturing processes conform to the environmental regulations of the country of origin.

LIBRARY OF CONGRESS CATALOGING–IN–PUBLICATION DATA

Royte, Elizabeth.
Bottlemania : how water went on sale and why we bought it / Elizabeth Royte.—1st U.S. ed.
p. cm.
ISBN-13: 978-1-59691-371-4
ISBN-10: 1-59691-371-1
1. Bottled water industry—Social aspects.   2. Bottled water—Social aspects.   I. Title.

HD9349.M542R69 2008
338.4'766361—dc22
2007052067

First U.S. Edition 2008

1   3   5   7   9   10   8   6   4   2

Typeset by Westchester Book Group
Printed in the United States of America by Quebecor World Fairfield

For Lucy, water lover.

CONTENTS

Chapter 1

AN ALARM IN THE WOODS

O<small>N A BALMY</small> fall afternoon, with the maples at their flaming peak and the white ashes shading to yellow, Tom Brennan, natural resources manager for Nestlé Waters North America, drives down a gravel road in western Maine. He parks his truck in front of a small stone cottage topped by a pitched green roof. The building wouldn't look out of place in the Adirondacks. But its green wooden door opens not to reveal a rag rug and a woodstove but yet another door—a serious-looking door made of thick steel that can be breached only with the right combination of keys, codes, and security cards. Behind it are cameras and a motion detector. Are they guarding a gold reserve or an arsenal? No, they superintend an assemblage of stainless steel pipes, gauges, levers, and a device called a pig, about the size and shape of a boat bumper, that's periodically forced through the pipes with water pressure to clean and disinfect. The linoleum floor is spotless.

"Any sort of intrusion into the pump house," Brennan says, "and the water automatically shuts off." The pump house aggregates water from five boreholes, or wells, located not far away at the bottom of a gentle valley, and sends it shooting through an underground pipe and, a mile to the north, into the largest water-bottling plant in the country. When the water comes back out, it's in plastic containers labeled Poland Spring.

I take a good look around, not really appreciating the engineering that goes into such a place, and then we turn to leave. I am eager to see the water, the place where it springs from the earth. Brennan fumbles with a security card and keys, then we continue downhill through a young forest. Turning a bend, we come upon a man in casual clothes walking rapidly, a roll of duct tape in his hand. His black Lab darts into the trees, then back out and in again. When he hears the truck, the hiker glances furtively over his shoulder, then slips into the roadside bracken.

"He sure disappeared quick," Brennan says, without emotion. Though the fifteen-hundred-acre property is private, Nestlé, a Swiss-owned conglomerate and the largest food-processing company in the world, isn't strict about trespassing. The road is gated but no fence lines the property. If hunters call first to make arrangements, they are welcome. But it isn't hunting season now.

At the bottom of the valley we park near five matching well houses, smaller versions of the stone building uphill. We walk into the woods and down a staircase flanked by white pine and larch. Where the slope bottoms out, tussock sedges line a shallow, sandy-bottomed raceway—narrow canals lined with boards. "The stream feeds into a trout hatchery," Brennan explains, pointing toward a shed in the distance. I walk along the watercourse, looking for springs. The ground is soft, and the water bubbles here and there through fallen leaves and watercress.

Finally I see what I am looking for. I squat in a patch of swamp dewberry and contemplate a tiny boil of water.

"Can I drink it?" I ask. Brennan shifts his weight and hesitates before saying, "If you want to." If I expect encouragement, it isn't forthcoming.

Filled with a sense of moment, I bend and dip my hand into the water, which appears black. I check to make sure there is nothing obvious swimming in my palm, then close my eyes and sip. "So this is it," I think. "I'm drinking from the source."

The water tastes good to me. It is cold—forty-five degrees according to Brennan—and it is fresh. It has no smell. Beyond that, I can say only that I feel privileged to be drinking straight from the ground, a rare possibility in this age of ubiquitous animal-borne diseases and pollution. I can choose from nearly a thousand types of bottled water on store shelves, but I can't, with infinitesimally few exceptions, drink from a naturally occurring body of water. Magically appearing from inside the earth, springwater has always had a powerful mystique. Civilizations have fought over such resources.

But I'm not feeling any mystique right now. What I'm mostly thinking as I sip anew is that this simple substance, rising in a rill not five hundred feet upstream from the Shy Beaver trout hatchery, is the driving force behind a multimillion-dollar plant that directs three hundred million gallons of water a year into the farthest reaches of New England, New York, and parts west. I try to stay focused on the moment, the elemental and pure (at least until it flows through Shy Beaver) nature of this liquid, but I can't help thinking that this water is so much more: a signature product of the world's largest food corporation, a flash point for activists environmental, religious, and legal, and either the biggest scam in marketing history or a harbinger of far worse things to come.

Brennan doesn't hurry me; he doesn't ask what I think of his water. He explains the morphology of the earth: the way glaciers retreated from this part of Maine thirteen thousand years ago and, in the process, formed deep beds of sand and gravel that expertly filtered the water. He shows me some test wells along the raceway and explains that water pumped through boreholes, the wells inside those little stone buildings, can be labeled *spring* if it has substantially the same chemical makeup as the actual spring, if it comes from the same geologic stratum as the spring, and if a hydraulic connection between the two can be proved. "And we did that," Brennan says.

We take a look inside one of the well houses—more security cameras, more spotless linoleum and gleaming pipes—then Brennan locks up and we head back up to the bottling plant. We're almost out of the woods when suddenly an electronic alarm shrieks through the silent forest. Rising from the valley floor, it drives crows from their treetops and brings my hands to my ears. *Whoop, whoop, whoop*—ten nerve-jangling blasts in a row, then a pause, then ten more. Brennan stomps on the brake and speed-dials the bottling plant, a look of mild panic on his face. Waiting for advice from HQ, he turns toward me and says, "You know all those caps getting screwed onto bottles that we just saw?" It's a blur to me, those half-liter containers moving around the plant at warp speed, more than five million containers a day, but I nod. "Well, all those bottles just stopped."

Maybe the alarm has something to do with that guy, the one with the duct tape and the Labrador? I ask. Or maybe security is simply testing the system? It isn't for Brennan to say.

"Why would someone want to mess with a pump house?" I ask as Brennan puts the truck back in gear.

"You'd be surprised," he says tersely. In 2003, operatives for the Earth Liberation Front (ELF) placed four incendiary devices inside a pump station in Michigan that supplied water to a Nestlé bottling plant. The devices failed to ignite, but ELF made its point: the substation was "stealing water," the group stated in a communiqué. Clean water, it continued, "is one of the most fundamental necessities, and no one can be allowed to privatize it, commodify it, and try and sell it back to us."

Is that what's happening here? I'd come up to the town of Hollis to see how the water gets out of the famous Maine woods and into the skinny bottles with the green labels. They are ubiquitous where I live. You can't walk a block in New York City without seeing a bottle in someone's hand, their baby stroller, or bike cage, spilling from the corner litter baskets or crushed flat and gray, ratlike, in the gutters. Nationwide, we discard thirty to forty billion of these containers a year. The bottles, and the trucks that deliver them, are haunting me. Poland Spring is the bestselling springwater in the nation, even in a city with some of the best tap water in the world. Everyone is drinking the stuff, and other waters like it. In the West, it's Arrowhead and Calistoga; in the South Central region, Ozarka; in the Midwest, Ice Mountain; in the mid-Atlantic, Deer Park; and in the Southeast, Zephyrhills—all owned by Nestlé, a company with estimated profits of $7.46 billion in

2006. Pepsi-Cola and Coke are bottling water too, and making billions.

Why this turn against the tap? And how had we gotten to the point where activists are sneaking bombs into pump houses—infrastructure devoted not to oil, but water? It isn't just Michigan: citizens in Wisconsin, Pennsylvania, California, New Hampshire, Texas, Florida, and, yes, even Maine, are in arms against ground-water pumping for bottling. Legal scholars are loudly debating water rights; the United Church of Canada has called for a North American boycott of the stuff, so has a group called Food and Water Watch. The Franciscan Federation declared to the Environmental Protection Agency that access to safe and clean water is "a free gift from God," and the National Coalition of American Nuns adopted a resolution, in the fall of 2006, that asked members to avoid drinking bottled water unless absolutely necessary. Their issue? Privatization of something so essential to life is immoral. An antiglobalization organization was traveling the country offering blind taste tests of bottled water versus tap. Their point—tap is pretty good—never fails to make the news.

Still, every week a new bottled water—offering the stuff neat or with "beneficial" additives (vitamins, herbs, laxatives, nicotine, caffeine, oxygen, appetite suppressants, aspirin, skin enhancers, or healing mantras)—hits the market. U.S. sales of bottled water leaped 170 percent between 1997 and 2006, from $4 billion to $10.8 billion. Globally, bottled water is a $60-billion-a-year business. In 1987, U.S. per capita consumption of the stuff was 5.7 gallons; by 1997 it was 12.1 gallons; and in 2006, according to the Beverage Marketing Corporation, it was 27.6. Sales of bottled water have already surpassed sales of beer and milk in the United States and by 2011 are, by some analysts, expected to surpass soda, of which Americans drink more than fifty gallons per person a year.

I've come to Maine because it seems an *unlikely* battleground. The state receives about forty-three inches of rain a year (about the same as other states in the region) and has a population of slightly more than one million, among whom Poland Spring is a familiar, and at one time beloved, face. The company has been bottling water from the town of Poland since 1845. Legal history recorded no objections when Hiram Ricker began to sell water from his family farm there, though a Portland newspaper, anticipating the nuns and the Canadians, scoffed at "selling something that God gave everyone for free." In recent years Poland Spring, which was bought by Perrier in 1980 and then Nestlé in 1992, has expanded its reach into other Maine aquifers, and the objections have been hard to miss.

The epicenter of Maine's water wars is Fryeburg, about an hour to the north of Hollis. "So what happened up there?" I ask Brennan, for the third time. We're sitting at the conference table in the bottling plant, which was built atop a former potato farm. The alarm out in the woods had, we just learned, been an electronic glitch—a relief to everyone. Now Brennan glances at me, and despite his efforts to stay on message, to stay upbeat, I can sense the man's fatigue. "Yeah," he says, with a downward cast of his eyes. "The infamous Fryeburg situation." He sighs. "It got complicated up there."

Fryeburg sits along Maine's western border with New Hampshire, a mere fifty-two miles northwest of Portland. The road in between passes ugly strip malls and tourist motels, busy marinas, and tiny towns with faded Main Street banners. Though Fryeburg, population three thousand, sees up to one hundred thousand canoeists and campers playing on its stretch of the Saco River in the summer, and twice that many visitors descend in October, for the eight-day Fryeburg Fair, the place has done little to attract the out-of-season day-tripper. Unlike neighboring towns to the east and west, Fryeburg has no book-shops, T-shirt stores, moose paraphernalia, or cappuccino joints. Instead, it has the Jockey Cap, a combo gas station and grill where older gentlemen sit on hard chairs reading the daily newspaper and the gossip flows all day. Near the town center is a small su-permarket, a culinarily depressing place. When I tell a local I bought an egg-salad sandwich at its deli counter, he physically recoils. The main drag features a bank, a few utilitarian stores, a smattering of private offices, and the Fryeburg Water Company, whose unprepossessing appearance, on the bottom floor of a two-story frame house, belies the company's position at the red-hot center of Fryeburg's multimillion-dollar water woes.

Fryeburg is old, established in 1762, and a little inbred: the same dozen names show up on buildings, parks, cemeteries, hills, and rosters of elected or appointed officials. I meet men who own mountains, miles of lakefront, and vast swathes of forest handed down by land grants from the governor of Massachu-setts. I hear about strangers showing up in town to buy property and the water that flows under it. Before long, Fryeburg seems like *Chinatown*, the movie, to me. Everywhere I turn there is in-trigue, there is someone with a heated opinion, with "water on the brain," as Jake Gittes, the character played by Jack Nicholson, puts it. I hear about hydrogeologists drilling test wells on the q.t., about dummy corporations, secret planning-board meetings, tape recorders at public meetings that stop at convenient times, notes that go missing, and appointed officials suspected of shilling for outside corporate interests. I meet the man who provided access to the spring that fills the tanker trucks of Nestlé.

And that, admits Howard Dearborn, was a big mistake.

When I first meet Dearborn, he is eighty-eight years old. His hair is snowy white, he wears oval, wire-rimmed glasses, and he dresses in timeless L.L. Bean fashion, his red-plaid shirt tucked into high-waisted chinos. A retired engineer, Dearborn lives alone in a sprawling split-level home amid a grove of white pines and beech on the shores of Lovewell Pond, not far from the center of Fryeburg. Though Dearborn has lived here for more than fifty years, locals still consider him an outsider: he's "from away." He sold the company he founded here, Dearborn Precision Tubular Products, fifteen years previously, and has filled his time since then running a private foundation, inventing mechanical tools, and, more recently, badgering Poland Spring, challenging its right to draw water, to truck it through town, and to remove it from the state.

While some water activists are concerned with truck traffic in their rural towns, and others focus on the morality of selling water for large profits, Dearborn's "big bitch," as he puts it, is that Nestlé is "ruining the lake" by pumping from the springs that feed it.

"The lake is dead now!" Dearborn says to me, in a tone that implies this is obvious. "The water stays in it too long because it's not being flushed by Wards Brook. It's warmer and there's increased growth of weeds on the bottom, which has lowered property values." Houses have been taken off the market because they didn't sell, Dearborn says. He worries that soon the pond will resemble Brownfield Bog—a low area that forms the southern end of Lovewell.

The heart of the two-thousand-acre Wards Brook drainage basin is the Wards Brook aquifer, made up of hundred-foot layers of permeable sands and gravel. It drains an area south of town, flowing north and then east into Lovewell Pond. Since 1955, the investor-owned Fryeburg Water Company has pumped water from the aquifer and piped it to nearly eight hundred customers in town, plus roughly seventy over the state line in East Conway, New Hampshire. Then in 1997, Hugh Hastings, president of the water company, paid a visit to Howard Dearborn.

"He stood on my deck," Dearborn says as he gestures over an array of bird feeders fattening the squirrels, "and he told me the town was growing and that he needed more water." Hastings had pointed out to Dearborn the tracts of forest the Hastings family owned: across the lake, to the northeast, was Mount Tom, which Hastings had recently sold to the Nature Conservancy; and around to the south was Pleasant Mountain, of which he and his family, which includes a state senator, own half. ("The Hastingses are like the Magnificent Ambersons," a conservation worker from the region tells me.) Eventually, Hastings got to the point of his visit: he asked Dearborn for a right-of-way through his property so that he could drill a second well, near his first, in the Wards Brook aquifer.

"And like a dumb ass I let him cut a road through my property," Dearborn says, shaking his head. "I even helped him out with my bulldozer."

Years passed, and then, in 2004, Dearborn read something in the local paper about Poland Spring attempting to build a bottling plant in Fryeburg. He and others began to ask themselves, "Is there that much water here?" Few had been paying much attention to the tanker trucks rumbling through town. Now, a citizens group from Hiram, through which trucks passed en route to the bottling plant in Hollis, counted ninety-two trucks in twenty-four hours. It happened seven days a week. In 2005, the company took more than 168 million gallons of water out of Fryeburg.

Where was that water coming from? The well near Dearborn's property, it turned out. "I thought Hugh wanted that water for the town of Fryeburg, not for Poland Spring," Dearborn says today, furious at the memory. Curiously, the Fryeburg Water Company doesn't sell the water to Poland Spring: that would be legal but it wouldn't be profitable. Maine's public utility commission forbids the water company from selling water at a price higher than it charges its town customers. Instead, the water is pumped by the water company and sold to a recently formed entity called Pure Mountain Springs for less than a penny a gallon. Pure Mountain Springs, now once removed from the PUC's price cap, turns around and sells the water to Poland Spring for four cents a gallon more. Who is Pure Mountain Springs, this ingenious middleman? It is Eric Carlson, a hydrogeologist who lives downstate, and John Hastings, the water company's superintendent and a son of Hugh.

Across the United States, surface water—the ocean, ponds, and rivers—are held in common as part of the public trust. But groundwater falls under different rules, depending on the state. Maine operates with a rule called absolute dominion, which it adopted in the late 1800s, a time of hand pumps and little understanding of the connection between groundwater and surface waters. The law grants landowners complete autonomy to take as much groundwater as they please. In Texas, the only other state in the nation that still follows the absolute dominion rule, they call it the law of the biggest pump. Other states use either the rule of prior appropriation (first in time, first in right); the rule of "reasonable use," which considers other usages and the wants of the community; or the rule of "correlative rights," which requires that all landowners above an aquifer share the resource. Absolute dominion is the weakest of all four groundwater protection rules, and it lets Hugh Hastings pump all the water he wants.

But the Fryeburg Water Company and Pure Mountain Springs aren't the only companies sticking straws into the Wards Brook aquifer. Across the street and upstream from the Fryeburg Water Company's wells, Rick Eastman owns a large plot of land on which he runs a plant nursery. In 2004, he and a local cabinetmaker named Jeff Walker dug a well on Eastman's property, formed the WE Corporation, and began selling water to a bottler they won't name (it isn't Poland Spring). By 2006, around eight hundred thousand gallons a day were flowing out of the Wards Brook aquifer into tankers and into town pipes. Meanwhile, Howard Dearborn's well, in the woods behind his house, was intermittently sucking air, for which he blames overzealous commercial pumping. More and more Fryeburg residents are concerned not only with the future quantity and quality of their drinking water, but also with the impact of pumping on the environment. What's happening to the aquatic organisms, the plants, and the other creatures that depend on flow from these springs? Others are asking if the desires of a multinational corporation should trump the wishes of the local community.

These frustrated citizens are doing all they can think of to stop the water juggernaut. A small group accused the town's planning board of being in Nestlé's pocket; they tried (but failed) to decommission its members. A former state legislator is lobbying to impose a tax on large commercial groundwater withdrawals in Maine. Poland Spring, after failing to buy significant tracts of land over the Wards Brook aquifer, bought land in the adjacent town of Denmark, where it hopes to pump 105 million gallons of water a year, send it through a pipeline to East Fryeburg, and load it into tanker trucks bound for the plant in Hollis. The multistage plan hit a wrinkle, however, when the town's board of appeals retracted its approval for the truck-loading station. Nestlé, which had been playing nice with Fryeburg so far, donating money to a local school and the recreation department, spun around and took the town to court. Now neighbors aren't talking to one another; some residents are boycotting the library, because it's headed by a staunch Nestlé opponent; legal fees are piling up; and more than a hundred thousand dollars has been spent on independent water reports. "You can't shake a stick without hitting a hydrogeologist in this town," the town manager tells me when I ask for one of these reports.

Fryeburg is tied up in fits. Its abundance of fine water has cast its unwitting residents into the middle of a social, economic, and environmental drama. The characters I meet begin to take on a Shakespearean aspect: there are seers and clowns, learned counselors and crooked leaders, scientists, scapegoats, and mercenaries. The stage is grand: vast swathes of rich farmland encircled by a sinuous river, mossy-banked springs linked to fathomless underground pools. Incomplete knowledge drives the town's water narrative: no one can say for sure how much water lies beneath Fryeburg or what removing it will do. No one can say for sure which of the town wells supplies Poland Spring, versus the town, at any given time. No one knows for sure the relationship between town gatekeepers and Nestlé Waters. And so bad feelings spread like a miasma.

Why would water arouse such ire in a place that has so much of it? Water wars have long been a staple of the arid West, where big dams impound the stuff, agriculture sucks up the lion's share, and secondary users scramble for what's left. For more than fifty years, prognosticators have predicted that Western rivers and aquifers would shrivel, and Westerners would soon be importing water from distant regions. In Maine, by contrast, dams are coming down to restore stream flow and salmon runs. Timber companies, landowners, and, more recently, conservation groups have protected millions of acres of forests in the upper watersheds. The state recently suffered a year of drought, but no one went thirsty. Maine doesn't have an enormous amount of rainfall, but it does have, in certain places, the sort of geology and forested watersheds that produce exceptionally pure water.

The hydrogeological facts combined with weak groundwater rules have made Fryeburg a perfect example of water's shift from a public good to an economic force. And it raises some thorny questions: Is it right to trade water at all, to move it from its home watershed to other states, or even countries? Should the taxpayers who protect land and water share the profits of those who pump and sell that resource? How is water different from such resources as oil, trees, or lobsters? The world population is growing rapidly, and fresh, drinkable water, most of which is stored in underground aquifers, is growing scarce. Groundwater pumping has already dried up rivers in Massachusetts, Florida, and other states. According to Robert Glennon, author of *Water Follies: Groundwater Pumping and the Fate of America's Fresh Waters*, "The United States is heading toward a water scarcity crisis: our current water use practices are unsustainable, and environmental factors threaten a water supply heavily burdened by increased demand."

So it goes, the world over. We may be the water planet, Blue Earth, but most of our water is salty; only 3 percent is fresh, and of that fraction only a third is available for human use. The rest is locked up in snowcaps and ice fields. Today, more than a billion people lack sufficient access to safe water. The United Nations projects that by 2025, increases in population and pollution, combined with drought and the reduced recharge of groundwater, will leave two out of three people in similarly dire straits. Those two out of three won't just be thirsty: already, some 5.1 million people a year die from waterborne diseases, many of which stem from lack of sanitation and its resulting water pollution. That number is going to spike.

Already, parts of Australia and the Middle East are running out of water; Mexico City is sinking as overpumping depletes its aquifer; 80 percent of surface waters in China and 75 percent in India are polluted beyond use. Here in the United States, the EPA projects that thirty-six states will experience water shortages by 2013. The Southeast and the Southwest are in severe drought now; New Mexico has a ten-year supply of water; Arizona is already importing everything it drinks. It stands to reason that the waters of Maine and other water-rich states will become ever more valuable. The prospect thrills those who own land atop pristine aquifers, but it terrifies many others.

Because water is so important to life—and commerce—it's been a cause of conflicts and a source of power since before the written word. (The word *rival* is from the Latin *rivalis*, meaning "one using the same stream as another.") The ancient Greeks, Romans, and Assyrians used water as a military tool and target, poisoning wells and destroying irrigation canals; through the 1870s, ranchers, farmers, and villagers in the desert of Southwest America fought violently over water rights; water shortages lie behind much of today's conflict in Darfur, though the recent discovery of an ancient underground lake in the region is expected to ease the misery. Meeting water needs and demands, says the Pacific Institute, a nonpartisan think tank that keeps a thirty-one-page timeline of these conflicts, "will never be free of politics."

Sure, the fuss in Fryeburg seems to be of far less import than battles over access to Assyrian irrigation canals or the damming of the Tigris River for military purposes. But it isn't. Today's struggle may lack spears and guns (so far), but in fifty years we may look back at the campaign to control Maine's groundwater as a defining moment in history. This is what modern water conflict looks like: neighbors fighting with neighbors, little towns fending off major corporations, life savings handed over to attorneys, interminable public meetings, property values gone to hell, dried-up or contaminated wells, and too many plants on the bottom of your pond. Every time I see a Poland Spring bottle—or a bottle of Evian, Fiji, or Voss—on my street in New York, I am reminded that real people live near its source, its tanker station, bottling plants, and the roads that lead to the highways that bring the water to me. Quite a lot of them aren't happy to have lost their say, to an outside corporation, over a resource so essential to their lives.

How did bottled water become so popular in the first place? And is it popular for good reasons or bad? What does it mean that we are abandoning municipal supplies? Twenty years ago, bottled water was a niche market, and the United States had no large-scale water-bottling industry. Today, of course, those bottles fill not only the shelves of gourmet stores (at Whole Foods, bottled water is the number-one item, by units sold) but also those of the A&P. They are ubiquitous in vending machines, at newsstands, and in gas stations. Our cars, StairMasters, and movie-theater seats have been redesigned to accommodate them. Altogether, more than seven hundred domestic and seventy-five imported brands are sold in the United States. The water comes from wells, springs, glaciers, icebergs, and rain, and from under the seafloor. Does this make it a preferable alternative to tap? Is bottling water sustainable? How does it help or hurt our world?

Even at the very start of my water investigations, I can see that I'll be dealing with two sets of questions. One has concrete answers: what are the physical differences between tap water and bottled, and what is water bottling actually doing to the environment and to local communities? The other questions are more abstract: Even if bottled water makes sense, for health or other reasons, even if it is harmless, is it ethical to profit from its sale? If we believe water is a basic human right—such as freedom from persecution or equality before the law—then why would we let anyone slap a bar code on it?

Chapter 2

ALL YOU CAN DRINK

I MAKE A COLD call and invite Michael Mascha to lunch in New York City. Mascha is a bottled-water expert, a bottled-water snob, in fact. Forced by his doctor to give up drinking alcohol roughly ten years earlier, Mascha ran hard in the other direction, embracing fancy water and starting a Web site for "bottled water connoisseurs." He'd recently written a book called *Fine Waters: A Connoisseur's Guide to the World's Most Distinctive Bottled Waters*, which I carry with me as I shop for something to pour him.

Since the weather is cloudless and warm, I decide we should eat and drink alfresco, in Manhattan's Bryant Park, on Forty-second Street. Mascha doesn't know it (he's Austrian and lives in Texas), but the park holds an important place in New York City's water history. More than 160 years ago, the city dammed the Croton River, in Westchester County, and sent its sweet waters forty-one miles through an aqueduct and pipes to a receiving reservoir in what is now Central Park. From there, the Croton flowed into an enormous distributing reservoir that stood right here, on Forty-second Street—at the time a pastoral hinterland. Decorated with Egyptian motifs, the reservoir covered four acres, with walls fifty feet high and twenty-five feet thick. To the west of the reservoir was Reservoir Square, which had been converted to a park from a potter's field. In 1884, this patch of land got yet another name, Bryant Park, in honor of the recently deceased poet and editor William Cullen Bryant.

From our spot near the southern edge of Bryant Park, Mascha and I would have had a great view of the reservoir, had it not been torn down in the 1890s to make way for the formidable New York Public Library, upon which we gaze today. Refurbished after a long period of neglect, Bryant Park is now one of the nicest, if most crowded, places to eat lunch in midtown Manhattan on a sunny afternoon.

I spend a shocking amount of time preparing for my date with Mascha. I pore through *Fine Waters*, searching for a range of brands to sample. Then I phone half a dozen stores, looking for one that sells them all. Impossible. When the big day arrives, I go on a spree, buying seven waters at three groceries. The bottles are heavy, and my conspicuous consumption makes me feel like a jerk—for reasons I'll get to later. But at the same time I'm excited. Maybe it is the fancy shops I visit (Dean & DeLuca, Whole Foods, and an upscale deli) or maybe it's the bottles themselves, from exotic locales, so nicely colored and shaped. Somewhere, a brand manager is pinching herself.

But what food will I pair with our waters? The thought of eating anything at all grosses me out, just a little. What can we possibly have that won't sully the purity of the water experience? Food seems base and heathen compared to the stuff in these bottles. A quick call to Mascha allays my fears. He doesn't care what we eat. "The whole idea is to enjoy the food and the water together," he says. "It's an experience, not a temple."

It used to be so much simpler. Water, essential for human, plant, and animal life, is the simplest beverage in the world. Since modern humans appeared, about 150,000 years ago, water has been our basic drink: we imbibe it before we're born, we beg for it on our deathbeds. Though people can live for weeks without a bite of nourishment, no one can live longer than a week without water, and even fewer days in an arid environment.

From the beginning of human time, access to sufficient clean water was the sine qua non for the establishment of a settlement. Lack of good water cramped expansion, and the search for new sources drew civilization's map. Waterborne diseases could wipe out entire communities, so fresh springs were protected and fiercely defended. In short, water acted as an evolutionary force.

Large cities must always have more water: they can't grow without it, and they always find ways to get it. Though it took interference by the U.S. Supreme Court, California got its hands on the Colorado River; Boston took water from the Connecticut River; and New York City captured water not only from rivers upstate but also from communities in New Jersey, Pennsylvania, and Delaware.

After finding water, cities had to protect it—from contamination, and from rivals. They had to store water for future use, and they had to move it around. The Egyptians, Persians, and Chinese figured out how to dig deep wells as early as 2500 BCE, and sophisticated water-storage systems were built in the Mesa Verde region of the American Southwest and in Syria by 2350 BCE. As early as 3000 BCE, the ancient Egyptians used aqueducts to move water to cultivated fields and to villages for drinking, washing, and controlling fires.

The Romans didn't start building their famous waterways until the ninth century BCE. But once they got going, they rocked. Over five hundred years, the Romans constructed eleven aqueducts that ran for nearly 260 miles above and below Rome, delivering twenty-five million gallons of water a day. Each ended with a flourish, an elaborate fountain. The hoi polloi collected water from these public sources; richer Romans paid to bring pipes into their homes. It was a pattern, from public to private, that's becoming increasingly common today.

Anticipating Robert Parker's *Wine Advocate* by many hundreds of years, the Romans ranked their water. Springwater from the Aqua Marcia was among the best; muddy water from a lake north of Rome was among the worst. Even the best wasn't good enough for Emperor Nero, who directed his servants to first boil his water, then pour it in a glass and cool it in snow. Even today, freshwater—some of it from the same springs that flowed in ancient times—burbles continuously from public spigots around Rome. It's easy to grab a sip, though Romans are among the world's biggest consumers of bottled water. (As a nation, Italians drink the most, per capita, followed by the United Arab Emirates.)

How did the ancients carry their water around? Well, they probably weren't as obsessed with portable hydration as we are today, scarcely able to leave the house without a cylinder of water, and they weren't commuting long distances to work, school, or play. Pottery had been invented in 6000 BCE, but water could have been stored long before in pitch-lined baskets, hollowed-out trees, gourds, large shells, or vessels of woven grass. The Vikings held liquid in buckets made of driftwood, their staves held tight with baleen. Other cultures transported water in bags made of leather, or the stomachs and bladders of animals. I once watched a federal trapper carefully remove the bladder of a coyote he'd just shot. It was filled with urine, which he wanted to use in trapping, and he asked me to hold the softball-size organ while he reloaded his gun. I pinched the top of the thing closed and held it some distance from my leg. Within minutes, the thin, whitish tissue had hardened in the dry Utah air; I could have set the bladder down in a depression without spilling a drop.

As cities grew, it became important to collect more water faster. Engineers raised surface and groundwater using waterwheels and steam engines. As it went in the Old World, so it went in the New. Boston built the first colonial water supply in 1652: it consisted of a twelve-foot-square reservoir, gravity-fed from nearby springs and wells. The first pumped-water supply in America was completed in 1755 in Bethlehem, Pennsylvania. According to Gerard Koeppel's *Water for Gotham*, the ingenious system featured "an undershot wooden waterwheel, iron crankshaft, and three water-powered forcing pumps. The system sucked spring water through a lead and wood pipe to a water tower 320 feet away and ninety feet high, then distributed it by gravity to four cisterns." New York City was far behind: it would take nearly two hundred years of disease, destructive fires, and bad politics—starting when the Dutch landed in Manhattan—for the city to boast of a reliable source of clean water: the suburbs.

While New World cities built public supplies, rich folks in the Old World pursued private water. Since ancient times, mineral water—which contains dissolved substances such as salts, sulfur compounds, calcium, or magnesium—had been considered therapeutic. With the imprimatur of royal or noble patronage, mineral springs or pools were transformed, in late-eighteenth-century Europe, into fashionable destinations where visitors complaining of everything from kidney stones to constipation would "take the waters." Sometimes the mineral water was consumed, in which case the destination was called a well; sometimes the mineral water was bathed in, in which case the destination was called a bath. If the visitors did both—drank and bathed—it was called a spa; the word is derived from the Belgian town of Spa, which has offered hot thermal baths since the fourteenth century. It was a short step from offering guests water in situ to sending them home with water in a ceramic or glass container (glass bottles have been around for a long time: the Syrians invented them in 100 BCE).

By the mid-nineteenth century, railways were bringing the middle classes to spas, and technology had advanced to the point where containers could be manufactured and filled by machine. Evian, San Pellegrino, Vittel, Vöslauer, Borsec, and Spa had become brand names: bottled water, at least in the Old World, was now thoroughly commercialized.

And soon, regulated. By this point, it was no longer possible simply to slap a label on a bottle and sell it. Source owners had to prove their mineral content was stable over two years. Vittel made the cut in 1855, and in 1863, Napoléon III granted mineral-water status to a fizzy spring near Vergèze, France, where Hannibal, the great Carthaginian general, had rested with his army (and its horses and elephants) before heading on to Rome in about 218 BCE. Or so the legend goes. Today, the source is known as Perrier, a brand pivotal to the success of bottled water in America.

At precisely one o'clock my water expert arrives at Bryant Park. With a couple of sandwiches and a box of fancy cookies, I wait at a table near the mowed lawn. We shake hands and then I nervously lay out my wares: I have Voss, from Norway; Jana, from Croatia; Gerolsteiner, from Germany; Iceberg, from off the coast of Newfoundland; Ty Nant, from Wales; Sanfaustino, from Italy; Mountain Valley Spring, from Arkansas; and a plastic bottle of mystery water around which I've wrapped a sheet of white paper. I feel a little conspicuous, with my cloth napkins, wineglasses, and eight bottles of water. Almost everyone around us has just one, either Poland Spring or Fiji, which is sold at park kiosks. (I don't see a single reusable bottle among the hundreds in hand, nor do I see a recycling bin.) I ask Mascha if my display makes him self-conscious. He shrugs. "I'm used to it."

At tastings, it is normal to have ten to fifteen bottles. "You start with something that has a neutral pH and low minerality, then you move to a high-mineral-content water." Mascha will go on like this for the next two hours, talking about minerality, pH, TDS (for total dissolved solids), and the size of bubbles. "Sanfaustino," he announces, pouring from the green bottle that he's selected to start us off. "It has midlevel mineral content with small, fine bubbles. It's naturally carbonated, which is rare." I take a sip. "You feel a little structure in the water?"

"Yes," I say, I can feel the bubbles. Mascha had written something about effervescent water having evenly spaced bubbles. I have to ask, "How do you measure the distance between bubbles? Does someone actually do this?"

My water expert cuts me a rueful glance. "It's not scientific," he says, then changes the subject. "This water has lots of calcium—it's hard water. It's good for you."

"So I see," I say. The bottle's three labels mention calcium no fewer than ten times. I like the taste of the Sanfaustino, though I can't say why. It has more flavor than my tap water, to be sure, but Mascha is reluctant to help me out with any subjective descriptions. He likes to stick to the facts. Even in his book, he studiously avoids the windy language of wine tastings to describe what is in his mouth.

Instead, he lets the look of the water—its label and bottle—and the water's "story"—its history and aspirations—shape his impressions. Is the water a natural product, that is, bottled straight from the earth, or is it a commodity, by which he means processed water, such as Aquafina or Dasani? Those waters he considers a scourge on the fine-waters landscape. "Most people in America don't know or don't care that they're tap. Here, the scientific aspect of food is cherished; Americans are infatuated with technology. In Europe, they value food. High-end waters, with nice bottles and brands, tie into this concept."

For years, Mascha has been leaning on American bottlers to upgrade their image, but he doesn't get much traction. "I'm frustrated," he says now. "I say to these people, 'Get a designer, develop your brand.'" He isn't a big fan of Poland Spring's thin plastic bottles, which, because they are inexpensive, let Nestlé compete with purified waters that come from municipal supplies—waters that happen to be bottled, as he puts it, but aren't fine bottled waters.

I find this ironic, since Poland Spring actually has a pretty good story, every bit as authentic as the European brands. It involves an old-timey Maine farmer and his kidney stones, cured in the early 1840s by drinking from the family spring in the tiny town of Poland. Soon, ceramic jugs of his water were being shipped to Boston and west on wagon trains. A fancy inn was built atop the hill near the spring, and fancy visitors arrived to take steam baths and other therapeutic water cures.

All well and good, as stories go. But fashions changed, city water systems improved with the widespread use of chlorine, bottled water began to seem old-fashioned, the inn at Poland Spring burned, and Nestlé acquired the somewhat moribund company in 1992. Within a few years the springwater, now in plastic bottles, was edging its way into supermarkets far from the woods of Maine. (Meanwhile, the rebuilt inn has become what Arthur Frommer calls "America's cheapest resort.") Mascha likes the taste of Poland Spring but doesn't care for its plastic bottle, or for Nestlé's hard-nosed lobbying of the Food and Drug Administration (FDA)—which regulates bottled water as a food product—to allow water drawn from a borehole to be labeled *spring*. It isn't honest, Mascha thinks, and it devalues water that actually *is* collected from springs.

According to the FDA, springwater must come from an

underground formation from which water flows naturally to the surface of the earth. It may be collected through a borehole, instead of the actual spring, under certain conditions: the bottler must prove a hydraulic connection between the spring and the borehole; the water must have the same physical properties as the water from the spring; and the spring must continue to flow. The anti-borehole crowd believes these distinctions are too vague, and that boreholes—by pulling from too wide a zone with powerful pumps—can potentially suck in poorly filtered water and contaminants.

Then there's the anti–Poland Spring crowd, which claims some of the company's wells have no connection to a spring at all. (One Nestlé borehole in Florida is nearly five thousand feet from the actual spring—a necessity because of the region's unique geology, says Tom Brennan.) The company argues that collecting water from a borehole is more sanitary than collecting it from a spring because the water never comes in contact with the earth's surface.

Roused to take legal action, several small springwater bottling companies in 2003 initiated a class-action suit to get Nestlé to either abandon its boreholes or to change its Poland Spring labels, which didn't list spring sources. In 2004, Nestlé settled, agreeing to pay nearly eleven million dollars in discounts and giveaways to bottled-water consumers and to make various charitable contributions. The suit didn't settle whether Nestlé's water is spring or not: it settled only that the plaintiffs' attorneys would quit challenging the labeling. Other plaintiffs, with their own springwater to sell, continue to press on with similar lawsuits. All this legal wrangling could be avoided, says Bill Miller, president of the

National Spring Water Association, which represents small bot-tlers, if the FDA would only simplify its rule: "Springwater comes from a spring, and well water comes from a well."

There is another irony to the Poland Spring story. It was Perrier—Poland Spring's stepmother or cousin, depending on how you look at the corporate hierarchy—that had cracked open the U.S. market for bottled water and set it down the path to sales of more than ten billion dollars a year.

Remember that spring where Hannibal and his elephants rested? A French physician named Louis-Eugène Perrier, who specialized in mineral-water treatments, bought it from a local businessman in 1898. Setting aside his medical practice, Perrier focused his energies on developing a glass bottle with a her-metically sealed metal cap, something that would stand up to the bubbly pressure inside. While Perrier was seeking financial backing, a wealthy Brit named St. John Harmsworth crashed his car near Nîmes and ended up in the hospital. There, he tasted the sparkling water from Vergèze and, when he recov-ered, hunted down Perrier, who offered him a tour of the springs. Harmsworth was, according to an annoyingly sunny company history, "instantly smitten." Perrier leased and then sold the property to Harmsworth, who renamed the property after his new best friend.

Harmsworth had zero marketing experience but an uncanny sense of possibility. He could see that spas were falling out of fashion, but he also noted that the Brits were currently en-tranced with artificially carbonated soft drinks. He designed a green bottle shaped like an Indian exercise club, the kind he'd used to strengthen his arms after the automobile accident; the shape would become as unique to bottled water as Coke's shape is to soft drinks. He invented a slogan—"the champagne of table waters"—and, ignoring the French market for the time being, sent his little bottles to the British army in India. The military endorsed the product, and Perrier went on to conquer thirst in the other British colonies, and then at Buckingham Palace. By 1908, Perrier was selling five million bottles a year.

Harmsworth died in 1933, with production at nineteen million bottles a year, and a group of British shareholders took over the company. After the war they sold Perrier to Gustave Levin, a Paris broker, who modernized the bottling plant and, in the late 1970s, reached across the Atlantic with six-million-dollars' worth of marketing schemes aimed at urban professionals— people like him. Investment bankers. Yuppies. Linking his product to health, he sponsored the New York City marathon (the tradition lives on: Poland Spring sponsors the race today). As Orson Welles purred on television ads, "There is a spring and its name is Perrier," sales went up and up, from twenty million dollars in 1978 to sixty million dollars the following year.

I haven't brought any Perrier today: it seems a little pedestrian, and I also have the feeling that Mascha doesn't much like it. His book says it contains "a very high level of nitrate" (which might come from fertilizer, animal waste products, decaying plant matter, septic tanks, or sewage treatment systems), and he gives it only three, of five, diamonds for *virginality*, a word used to mean distance from pollution. I didn't bring any Poland Spring either, knowing how Mascha feels about thin plastic bottles. Still, I think American water should be represented so I settle on Mountain Valley Spring, which is bottled near Arkansas's Hot Springs National Park. Mascha seems to have a soft spot for Mountain Valley: he likes its green glass bottles, its deep history, mineral content, and five-star virginity.

North Americans, well before the nineteenth-century spa craze introduced by European immigrants, weren't unfamiliar with mineral waters or healing springs. Records from the fourteenth century indicate the Iroquois, in upstate New York, were fans of Saratoga's springs, and in 1541 warring Tula Indians laid down their weapons, according to Spanish explorer Hernando de Soto, to sip the stuff that's now bottled under the Mountain Valley trademark. In California's Solano County, Tolenas Indians drank from mineral springs, one of whose waters would later be marketed as an early Viagra: "To those suffering from a loss of virile power, this beverage is an absolute blessing," read a pamphlet of the mid-nineteenth century. (It worked on malaria and hangovers too.) The Wappo Indians of the northern Napa Valley visited its geyser springs, which were eventually developed into the Calistoga Mineral Water Company, now owned by Nestlé.

In the postcolonial period, healing water reached its popular zenith following the Civil War as developers built European-style resorts and spas, appealing to class consciousness. With some bottlers claiming their water cured "kidney diseases, scrofula, salt rheum, erysipelas, dyspepsia, general debility, chronic consumption, catarrh, bronchitis, constipation, tumors, piles and cancerous affections," it was no wonder. Maine's own Poland

Spring was said to cure dyspepsia (aka indigestion) and liver complaint, though contemporary Nestlé literature says only that "drinking plenty of water" flushes toxins and impurities from the body, reduces daytime fatigue, nourishes skin, and relieves constipation. It's hard to argue with—or prove—that.

America had hundreds of regional bottled-water companies in the nineteenth and even twentieth century. But the bottlers focused, for the most part, on home and office delivery: they supplied offices with water for coolers. Single-serve water bottles, known in the biz as "packaged water," hadn't entered the public consciousness. All that changed with Perrier.

By 1988, the French company was selling three hundred million bottles a year; it controlled 80 percent of the imported water market and by 1989 had U.S. revenues of $110 million. Perrier's lighthearted TV ads, which had a lot of fun with bubbles, were ubiquitous. They gave American consumers the idea that a touch of luxury was not beyond their means. During this period, Perrier was the best-known mineral water in the world.

And then disaster struck: in 1990, a random check of Perrier bottles in North Carolina turned up traces of benzene. (A known carcinogen, benzene comes from both nature and industry. Ingesting it at high levels can cause stomachaches, sleepiness, convulsions, and death; the health effects from low levels are unknown. The EPA allows five parts per billion of benzene in drinking water; Perrier had between eleven and eighteen.) The company announced a worldwide bottle recall, and sales, predictably, plummeted. But crisis for one was opportunity for others. The bottled-water juggernaut was in motion,

Nestlé bought the wounded (but affordable) Perrier, and sales of non-Perrier water took off like, well, carbonated liquid squirting from a tiny hole.

It's important to note that hardly anyone was drinking bottled water because he or she was thirsty and distrusted what came out of the tap or fretted about the calories in other beverages. That would come later. Modern consumers first sipped Perrier, or Evian or Vittel, because it *signified*. Water, in this case, was a social—not just a physical—resource. Ordering imported water was classy; it improved the tone of a dinner party. Once that idea took hold in America, there was no going back.

Between 1990 and 1997, U.S. sales of bottled water shot from $115 million to $4 billion, boosted by public health messages against obesity, by multimillion-dollar ad campaigns that emphasized the perceived health benefits of bottled water, and by an unglamorous technological advancement: the invention of polyethylene terephthalate (PET) plastic. PET was cheaper, lighter, stronger, brighter, and clearer than the original polyvinyl chloride bottles; it was durable and, theoretically, recyclable. The introduction of the half-liter PET bottle in 1989 "revolutionized our industry," Kim Jeffery, president of Nestlé Waters North America, said. For the first time, people had an alternative to portable sodas. After Madonna adopted Evian as her house drink (and love object: she fellated a bottle in her film *Truth or Dare*), and photographers snapped pictures of models toting bottled water—they said it clarified their skin and suppressed their appetite—a liter of Evian became a bona fide fashion accessory.

And so it went, into the next decade. Drinking bottled water, like practicing yoga and eating organic food, was a station on the way to enlightenment. Advertisers used words (*pure, natural*) and imagery (waterfalls, mountains) to imply that bottled water tasted better and was healthier than tap. Some brands went even further. In 2006, ads for Fiji Water stated, "The Label Says Fiji Because It's Not Bottled in Cleveland." Annoyed, Cleveland officials tested the import and found 6.3 micrograms of arsenic per liter. City tap had none. (The EPA's maximum allowed level is 10 micrograms per liter.) Rohan Oza, a senior vice president of marketing at Glacéau, which makes distilled waters (in which water is boiled and then the condensed vapor is collected), told a business publication that Americans "are looking for products that make them feel better, physically, mentally, and emotionally."

I have to laugh when I read that because Glacéau makes *me* feel worse. I'm not drinking the stuff: it is the company's ads, which ask, "Who Approved *Your* Water?" The copy claims tap water is "rejected by Mother Nature"; springwater is approved by nature "for potty training animals" (accompanied by an ideogram of a fish pooping); and purified water is approved by the FDA, but "investigated by the FBI" (with an ideogram of a belching factory). Because I'm pretty sure the FBI doesn't investigate the quality of bottled water, I e-mail the company to find out more.

Mike, a consumer-relations representative, writes me back: "i am unfamiliar with the advertisement you are speaking of. however, our advertising is meant to be taken light heartedly. our goal is to communicate our products in a fun, irreverent and humorous way[.] if you have any questions or if I can be of further assistance, please don't hesitate to contact me. thank you again, and remember to drink better water!"

And drink a lot of it, Mike forgets to say. All the bottlers are now advising us to consume eight eight-ounce glasses of water each day. Their ads remind us the adult human body is 50–65 percent water (babies are even soggier, at 75 percent), and that dehydration can lead to seizures, then brain damage, then death. It sounds pretty serious. But is it true?

Though the maxim has become accepted wisdom, eight a day has never been scientifically proved. In fact, says Heinz Valtin, a retired Dartmouth Medical School kidney specialist, it makes little sense. Valtin spent a lot of time searching for the definitive source of the rule but discovered only that the Food and Nutrition Board of the National Research Council recommended adults drink approximately "1 milliliter of water for each calorie of food," which translates to roughly two to two and a half quarts per day (or sixty-four to eighty ounces). The report states, in its next sentence, that "most of this quantity is contained in prepared foods," though Valtin suspects few readers got that far. Digging further, the physiologist analyzed published surveys of healthy populations and found that most people weren't drinking that much. An enormous amount of scientific literature shows how well the body maintains water balance, he noted. "The body can't store water. If you have more than you need, you just pee it away."

Now, Valtin says, he's tired of trying to prove a negative. "I would argue further that for the time being the burden of proof that everyone needs eight by eight should fall on those who persist in advocating the high fluid intake without, apparently, citing any scientific support." Not only does food count for fluid intake (most of a cooked noodle's or rice grain's weight is water), medical scientists argue, so do caffeinated beverages and, in moderation, beer. Let thirst be your guide, says Dr. Simeon Margolis, professor of medicine and biological chemistry at the Johns Hopkins School of Medicine. (Unless you're elderly, says Roberta Anding, a clinical dietitian in adolescent and sports medicine at Baylor Medical College. "Thirst is one of the poorest-tuned defense mechanisms we have. The older you get, the less reliable that is. And athletes, of course, need even more than eight eight-ounce glasses a day.")

Drinking too much water can, though, be dangerous. In January of 2007, a Sacramento County, California, woman trying to win a Nintendo Wii on a radio program drank almost two gallons of Crystal Geyser without a bathroom break. She left the radio station with a headache, didn't win the Nintendo, and died that afternoon in her home. The condition, called hyponatremia but more frequently referred to as "water intoxication," causes blood levels of minerals and sodium to plummet. It can lead to brain swelling, seizures, coma, and then death. A college student died after a similar stunt, in 2005, as have athletes and teenagers after ingesting ecstasy, which brings on a powerful thirst.

I'm so caught up in this question of proper hydration that I start wondering if my daughter, Lucy, will do better on spelling tests if her brain—which is, like everyone's, 75 percent water— has more of it. I am convinced she drinks less than eight ounces a day, the amount she takes to school and then, mostly, carries home. There is no way her food provides the other seven cups. "I drink my water and then refill the bottle," Lucy tells me, but I have my doubts. I nag some more and, noting no change in her drinking habits, one morning mix eight ounces of water with two drops of red food coloring. I pour six ounces into her water bottle—it is opaque and red—and leave two ounces in a clear glass at home, as a control. It's taken me some time to devise this experiment, and I am looking forward to the results. If Lucy drinks and refills, the red won't match my control water; if she simply drinks, I can measure how much.

When I pick her up that afternoon, Lucy digs into her backpack and pulls out a one-line note from her teacher: "Lucy's water turned red today." Curses! Lucy explains, "I dripped some water on my desk and Ms. Barbara saw it and she told me to dump it out." I'm crushed. What are the odds Lucy would drip water today, and that her teacher would even notice? Now, not only can't I repeat the experiment (the Heisenberg Uncertainty principle, I tell Lucy), but her teacher thinks I'm nuts.

My next step is to buy a urine specific-gravity test, but before I can get to the drugstore, Lucy and I visit her pediatrician for a routine checkup. He glances at her tongue and says she's fine. But he has his doubts about me.

In 1994, Pepsi introduced its own water, called Aquafina, to the packaged-beverage market, and in 1999 Coke came out with Dasani. Both companies had taken some hits for pushing sugary, fattening drinks on kids and adults: getting into water was their way of maintaining their share of the lucrative beverage market. (More recently, these megacompanies have been buying up smaller beverage companies that make water and energy drinks; in 2007, Anheuser-Busch bought the right to distribute Icelandic Glacial water in the States, and Coca-Cola paid $4.1 *billion* for Glacéau. Obviously, they think the market for water is strong.)

Both Coke and Pepsi draw water from municipal sources—from city pipes in such places as Detroit, Wichita, Fresno, New York City, and Jacksonville—then filter the bejesus out of it (using a series of membranes and carbon filters) and sterilize it (with ultraviolet light and ozonation). Dasani adds back minerals, to give the water some body, and salts, for taste (just like fast food). Aquafina bottles its distilled water neat. For these brands, choosing a location with good infrastructure—a plant, access to large markets—is far more important than the quality of the water they start with.

In 2006, 44 percent of the bottled water sold in the United States came from municipal supplies and was labeled either *drinking water* or *purified water*. Every time I hear someone crow that Aquafina or Dasani is "just tap," that consumers are being ripped off, I want to shake him or her. I feel funny defending the multinational corporations, with their misleading marketing and high prices, but those brands, being filtered to the nth degree, are nothing like the stuff that flows from municipal pipes and out through kitchen faucets.

Taking advantage of their vast networks of soda-bottling plants, Coke and Pepsi can bottle water relatively close to where it is sold, which means it costs less to put Dasani and Aquafina on a grocery shelf than it does, say, a bottle of Poland

Spring, which has to be shipped from Maine. (Nor do Coke and Pepsi have to spend money collecting data from monitoring wells, protecting the virginity of their sources, or battling community opponents.) To compete with Coke and Pepsi, bottlers of springwater have to sell more product, and that means spending more on advertising.

In 2005, the bottled-water industry spent $158 million on advertising in the United States. If you're wondering why bottled tap water costs so much, here's one answer. In 2006, Pepsi spent more than $20 million on its "drink more water" campaign, which suggested that Aquafina would make those who drank it look and feel better. (According to news reports, $20 million is a typical budget for a bottled-water campaign.) It's no coincidence that most of these ads target fifteen- to thirty-four-year-old women, those most susceptible to fashion.

Coke and Pepsi have other advantages over regional or imported spring or mineral water. Since they already have supply deals with large retail chains, it's a simple matter to push their water into those stores, and into their branded vending machines in schools, stadiums, office buildings, and other public places. One exception is in New York City, where Pepsi has the contract for the Department of Environmental Protection's headquarters, in Queens. When the company began stocking its vending machines with Aquafina, DEP ordered the product out of the building. "We drink our own water here!" the agency scolded the company. Now the machines sell sodas, and sports and fruit drinks, and employees sip bits of Esopus Creek, one of the city's water sources in the Catskill Mountains, from water fountains bolted to the wall.

As if reaching out to retail customers weren't enough, Nestlé in 2002 produced a CD-ROM training manual called "Pour on the Tips," aimed at waiters. Converting just twenty guests per shift from tap water to bottled, said the CD, would bring in an extra hundred bucks, or more, a month. Waiters were taught to repeatedly fill fancy goblets nearly to the top with fancy water (in addition to Perrier, Nestlé also imports San Pellegrino, Contrex, and Acqua Panna), and to identify the table's "lead buyer." Then, to shame him or her. As waiter-turned-restaurant-consultant Bob Brown told the *Wall Street Journal*, "I say 'Would you like to have a couple more bottles chilled down?' Most of the time they say yes. It feeds their ego."

On the Waiter's Revenge Internet message board, a server who goes by the name Dollfinn wrote, "I get great pleasure out of making each of those ladies who are trying to impress their friends . . . repeat the word 'tap' back to me." Restaurants were advised to serve brands their customers wouldn't know from the supermarket shelves, the better to jack up their retail price. Bottled water has the highest markup of any item on a menu; or in a gas station mini-mart, for that matter. According to Andre van der Valk, who owns a Shell station in Los Angeles, "You tend to make at least fifty to sixty percent on a bottle of water. [It's] more profitable than gasoline." According to restaurant consultant Clark Wolf, the restaurant industry takes in between $200 million and $350 million from bottled water each year.

The outrageous success of bottled water, in a country where more than 89 percent of tap water meets or exceeds federal health and safety regulations, regularly wins in blind taste tests against name-brand waters, and costs 240 to 10,000 times less than bottled water, is an unparalleled social phenomenon, one of the greatest marketing coups of the twentieth and twenty-first centuries. But why did the marketing work? At least part of the answer, I'm beginning to understand, is that bottled water plays into our ever-growing laziness and impatience.

Americans eat and drink more on the run than ever before. The author Michael Pollan reports that one in three American children eat fast food every single day, and 19 percent of American meals and snacks are eaten in the car. Bottled water fills a perceived need for convenience (convenience without the calories of soda, that is): hydration on the go, with bottles that fit in the palm of the hand, in a briefcase or purse.

According to research conducted by the Container Recycling Institute (CRI), between 1960 and 1970 the average person bought 200 to 250 packaged drinks each year—mostly soda and beer—and many of those were in refillable bottles. When I was growing up, my family drank only from the faucet and from family-size containers. We quenched our thirst, when out and about, with water from public fountains. Either that, or we waited till we got where we were going. On picnics, we might have a big plastic jug of lemonade, homemade. Sure, the grown-ups occasionally bought beer, but the idea of single-serve beverages were considered, by and large, frivolous.

Today, the tap is alien to today's youth, who've grown up thinking water comes in bottles, taps aren't for drinking, and fountains equal filth. Kids like having their hands on a personal water bottle, but they have no interest in washing that bottle out, to be reused another day, or otherwise taking responsibility for their waste.

Stores selling water are on every corner, while drinking fountains or restaurants happy to fill a glass for free are increasingly rare. "As refillables were phased out, as technology developed to enable single-serving plastic bottles, and as industry marketing efforts were ramped up," CRI reports, "packaged beverage consumption grew and grew." The success of portable water in the nineties hinged on the mind-set, established in the seventies and eighties, that it was okay to buy—and then toss—single servings of soda while on the go. In 2006, Americans consumed an average of 686 single-serve beverages per person per year; in 2007 we collectively drank fifty billion single-serve bottles of water alone. An entire generation is growing up with the idea that drinking water comes in small plastic bottles. Indeed, committed tap-water drinkers are far more likely to be older than devoted bottled-water drinkers.

Like iPods and cell phones, bottled water is private, portable, and individual. It's factory-sealed and untouched by human hands—a far cry from the public water fountain. (Fiji exploits this subliminal germophobia with its slogan "Untouched by Man," as does a company called Ice Rocks that sells "hygienic ice cubes"—springwater hermetically packaged in disposable plastic.) Somehow, we've become a nation obsessed with hygiene and sterility. Never, outside of an epidemic, have we been more afraid of our own bodies. Supermarkets provide antibacterial wipes for shopping cart handles. Passengers bring their own linens to cover airline pillows. Supermarkets wrap ears of corn in plastic: corn still in its husk! (The downside, besides mountains of waste, is the development of superresistant bacteria immune to most of the commonly used antibiotics.)

In *Consumed: How Markets Corrupt Children, Infantilize Adults, and Swallow Citizens Whole*, Benjamin Barber argues that consumer culture has turned adult citizens into children by catering to our narcissistic desires and conditioning us to passionately embrace certain brands and products as a necessary part of our lifestyles. Is it narcissism that pulls people into stores the second they feel thirsty? Or is it a need for emotional succor? City dwellers walk down the street swigging; they stand in conversation and mark time with discreet sips. You see it in lines at the movies and in cars on the freeway. (But only in the United States, Mascha says. "In Europe, no one walks down the street sucking on a bottle of water. We wait and we have a nice meal.") Surely these people have access to water at the end of their journey and are in no danger of desiccating on the spot. No, this is water bottle as security blanket.

It doesn't take Mascha long to realize he is walking into the belly of the beast, drinking bottled water with me. On the phone before we met, I admitted I knew nothing about "fine waters," let alone the cheap stuff. I consumed none of the 27.6 gallons that the average American drinks annually, and I felt like an ostentatious jerk buying all that fancy stuff for my meeting with Mascha. I'd never even tasted Poland Spring until my first visit with Tom Brennan in Hollis, Maine. We'd been talking in the conference room when plant manager Bill Maples swept in bearing swag for all: eight-ounce bottles of water. I had my own, I said to Maples in what I hoped was a jocular tone, and pulled out my Nalgene, a wide-mouthed bottle made of polycarbonate plastic. I'd filled it that morning from a sink in Yarmouth, Maine, which has excellent water.

Maples handed me a bottle anyway and snapped his open. I unscrewed the blue top of my Nalgene. In this light, and next to the sparklingly transparent Poland Spring bottle, my container looked dull and yellow, like old toenails. The threads in the screw top weren't so clean. Taken aback, I asked myself, "How old is this thing? And when was the last time I sterilized it?" The answers were "About a decade" and "Never." Still, I wanted to make a point. I wasn't a bottled-water customer. While they drank their company's product, I took a sip of Yarmouth, and the water tasted fine. Or maybe it just tasted like what I was used to.

The truth is, I didn't want to drink Poland Spring because I didn't want to like it. I was almost certain it would taste better than Yarmouth water, which contains chlorine and comes through pipes never visited by a disinfecting pig. But so what? Foie gras tastes better than chopped liver. That doesn't mean I'm going to buy it. I don't need to spoil myself. I don't want to get used to expensive things, especially things that might, if the nuns and greenies are right, disrupt the social and environmental order.

I might have been overintellectualizing this, but I worried that drinking bottled water would only contribute to an insidious trend. It was becoming normal to pay high prices for things that used to cost little, or nothing. Such as television reception (now we have expensive cable). Or basic telephone service (now we have cell phones). The shifting baseline means that instead of collectively fighting problems—such as bad service or bad quality—we accept them and move on: to the private sector. The city of Baltimore, after fifteen years of trying to remove lead from public schools' water fountains, in 2007 gave up and switched to coolers of bottled water.

The environmental writer Bill McKibben calls this movement away from a sense of common purpose and toward personal enhancement "hyperindividualism." It puts earbuds in our ears and divorces us from communal experience; it builds bigger houses and bigger cars, while it clogs the roads and warms the climate. Hyperindividualism is relatively new, McKibben writes, "but very powerful." And while having more personal stuff signals strong economic growth, it ain't making us happy, according to some economists and sociologists. In fact, it's increasing social alienation. Hyperindividualism lets those who can afford to opt out—whether from public schools, mass transit, or tap water—to further isolate themselves, in style. A 1985 article in the *Financial Times* declared that buying bottled water "represents the exercise of private choice in preference to public provision, which can seriously be seen as a good in itself." Why? Because public provision can be inefficient, inadequate, or unhealthy.

I talked to Brennan and Maples for several hours with the Poland Spring bottle in front of me. The men sipped from their containers and I from my Nalgene. Finally, like a dieter sitting in front of a popcorn bowl, I'd had enough: I just had to sample their water. I cracked the top—pop! I liked that sound; everyone did—and took a careful sip. And you know, it really did taste good—round and smooth. But, as I said, it wasn't something I wanted to get used to. I closed the top and set the bottle aside.

Mascha and I have tried six waters by now, though he has little to say about any of them. Me either, except for the Gerolsteiner, which has big bubbles and a salty, chalky taste that I like. The king daddy of mineral water, which by law contains at least 250 parts per million of naturally occurring total dissolved solids, Gerolsteiner clocks in with a TDS of 2,527. It has the usual calcium and magnesium, plus chloride, fluoride, bicarbonate, manganese, nitrate, potassium, silica, sodium, strontium, and sulfates.

The spring and artesian waters (which are pumped from an aquifer but not from a spring) I selected don't make much of an impression on me. Are they pure, crisp, refreshing—the words most commonly used to describe water (and beer)? Sure. But what does *pure* mean? "I never use that word," Mascha says. "There's always something in there." He pours a sample of Voss, which has a TDS of twenty-two, and says, "This is pretty much what rainwater tastes like. It would be good with sushi." I have no opinion of the water, but the bottle is kind of cool—a straight-sided tube with a wide, gray cap.

We're pouring smallish portions and dumping what we don't want onto the Bryant Park plantings, feeding Old World rain to the rootlets of New World shrubs. I decant a few inches of Iceberg water into Mascha's glass. "Classic rainwater," he says, after a quick sip. It too has a low TDS. Mascha isn't a fan. Icebergs contain a gazillion layers of compressed snow, some of which fell during the Industrial Revolution, when the air over cities was black with soot, and some during the 1950s, when atomic tests put radioactive particles into the atmosphere. Iceberg water is made by chunking off bits of berg using a crane, then crushing, melting, and storing it in a tank inside a barge.

Mascha seems to be fading: perhaps he is waterlogged. It's time to open the mystery bottle. I crack the top and pour a little into our glasses. "You go first," he jokes. I do; then he sips and asks, cocking his head, "Is this distilled?"

"Um, no, I don't think so," I say. "But it's been through several other processes." I wait for Mascha to try another sip, to offer some expert insight.

"It's not Le Bleu, is it? Le Bleu is triple-distilled."

"Nope," I say. Mascha seems uninterested in taking another taste, or in further speculation. So I reveal, "Actually, this stuff is bottled at a wastewater treatment plant in Singapore. They run the effluent through all kinds of microfilters and reverse osmosis and then treat it with UV light. They call it NEWater."

Mascha gives me an odd look.

"So what do you think?" I say.

"I'm feeling a little queasy."

"I think it smells musty," I offer. He sniffs his glass, shrugs, and sniffs mine. He isn't getting musty from the water. "Another sip?" I say. He shakes his head vehemently.

"People taste water and they use all this flowery description," he says. "A week later they drink the same water and they think it tastes different. These are not repeatable experiences: it's the same with wine." Humans rely on many cues when they taste, he continues, which is why a product's story is so important. He doesn't have NEWater's story, and so he says nothing. Later, I give him a bit more of its story—Singapore's ultra-treated wastewater is mixed in a reservoir with freshwater in a ratio of one to ninety-nine, and it seems to sit quite well with Singaporeans who drink it daily from the tap. I got my bottle of NEWater from a friend who'd recently toured the plant, where they give away samples of the stuff uncut with any freshwater: it's 100 percent reclaimed. Armed with this knowledge, Mascha still dismisses the product as "unexciting."

"Are you kidding?" I nearly shout. The story has technology, psychology, politics. It comes from a country so enthralled with order that it fines citizens for jaywalking, spitting, and failing to properly flush the toilet. It galls me that Mascha prefers a water like Bling—which comes in a corked bottle decorated with Swarovski crystals. Three quarters of a liter sells for forty dollars in stores or ninety dollars at nightclubs.

"Bling is extremely interesting," Mascha asserts. "The water is from English Mountain spring in Tennessee, but the bottle is the main event. It personifies Miami, Las Vegas, and Los Angeles. It shows that water can be as desirable as a bottle of Cristal champagne. You go to a club, you order Bling to impress your underage girlfriend." He insists Bling has *terroir*, because it has contact with geological features, but he won't admit that NEWater, which has contact with millions of Singaporeans, has an equally exciting story.

I give up: Mascha will never see it my way.

By now I'm getting a sense of why bottled water has become such a success in this country. Marketing persuaded Americans that the store-bought stuff was natural and pure, which complemented our ideas about personal well-being. We were convinced that if you cared about your health, you needed to drink at least eight glasses of water a day, which meant that portability was essential. We suspected that drinking tap water was déclassé, and that municipal water supplies were neither natural nor pure, let alone crisp and refreshing.

But what's in tap water, really? I'm eager to find out, since I drink it day and night, but first I have an appointment back in Maine, to check out the "infamous" Fryeburg situation.

Chapter 3

MYSTERIES OF THE DEEP

O N A W A R M October morning, I meet Miles Waite on Howard Dearborn's sandy beach. Lovewell Pond looks like black glass, and it's ringed with beeches, paper birch, and red maples, whose brilliant yellow and orange canopies reflect jaggedly along its shore. We load some equipment aboard a skiff, which Dearborn himself built, and shove off. This is Waite's fourth visit to the pond, and the hydrogeologist, who is based in Burlington, Vermont, is here to collect yet another round of samples and readings. Dearborn is certain the lake's flora and fauna have changed since Poland Spring came to town, and that the "aquafire"—as he pronounces it—is depleted. He hired Waite to produce the evidence to prove it.

At the first sample station, which he locates with a GPS, Waite measures the elevation of the lake bottom and its temperature, then starts filling an assortment of bottles with water. Lab technicians will analyze them for chlorophyll a, orthophosphorus, total phosphorus, Kjeldahl nitrogen, and E. coli. At the second sample station, Waite takes a deep sample with a Van Dorn bottle. He shows me a capsule the size of a small fire extinguisher on a wire tether. Both ends are open; when the bottle hits the lake bottom, Waite releases a lead weight that slides down the wire and smacks into a release button, which traps a water sample inside. Next comes a reading with a pressure-sensitive thermometer. "Fifty-five point seven degrees at thirty-eight point eight feet," Waite drones, logging the numbers on a form. Except when Waite walks from bow to stern, the boat is motionless. "Last time we were out here it was all whitecaps," he says.

The summer before, Waite and his team had collected sediment with an Ekman grab sampler, another spring-loaded gizmo that trapped a handful of lake-bottom sediment. A lab analyzed its total phosphorus and total organic carbon, and it ran a grain-size analysis. The choices were gravel, sand, silt, or clay. "And what was it?" I ask.

"It was sand, with some silt. This tells you the potential for plant growth; plants don't do well in coarse sand." A colleague of Waite's was studying the lake's vegetation; Waite also had data on turbidity, or the amount of suspended sediment in the lake, gleaned from a machine called a nephelometer, which beams light through water and measures how much of it reflects off suspended particles onto a light detector. In previous Lovewell Pond studies, researchers collected data on water transparency using a Secchi disk—a black-and-white plastic circle lowered on a measured string. It works like this: from the shady side of the boat, lower the disk. When you can't see the disk anymore, write down the corresponding number on the string, indicating depth. Voilà.

A few months ago, Dearborn had photographed rafts of submerged plant fronds and sent them to Tom Brennan, basically blaming the pond's excessive plant growth on his company's appetite for groundwater. Brennan thanked Dearborn for the pictures and wrote, "You may have milfoil." Milfoil is an invasive plant introduced into Maine lakes by careless boaters. Dearborn wrote back, "I am sorry that you seem to be having an eye problem! . . . Maybe your Optometrist can cure your 'seeing things that are not there' problem." Dearborn believes the plants are native, and they bolted because of excess nutrients in the lake.

Gene Bergoffen, who lives on the lake about a mile and a half down from Dearborn, is the president of the Lovewell Pond Association, and the chairman of the town's planning board. He sees things differently. "I know of no specific environmental concerns with the lake," he tells me. "Howard's argument, that cool water from the stream is reduced and so changes the temperature in the lake—I don't buy it."

The Wards Brook aquifer, which provides only a small portion of the water to Lovewell Pond relative to surface water input from Wards Brook and the Saco (which provides the lion's share during spring flood) is perhaps the best-studied aquifer in Maine. Formed by an ancient glacial lake, the deep basin of sand and gravel is a factory for producing exquisitely filtered water: it has a storage capacity of eight billion gallons. But how much of that can be pumped before the ecosystem is changed? An early modeling study of the aquifer, funded by Poland Spring, concluded that the current level of pumping—nearly eight hundred thousand gallons a day, between the town pump and two commercial extractors—was sustainable. Still, its authors recommended further study of the area's hydrology. Next came a firm, hired by the town of Fryeburg, which at first proposed looking at both Wards Brook and the pond, but later removed all but a tiny part of Lovewell from its purview. Dearborn objected, the town shrugged, and Dearborn hired his own hydrogeologist.

It would be easy to dismiss Howard Dearborn as a crank—and some do. But the level of his well and the plant growth in his pond speak to far larger issues in Fryeburg and around the world. Are large-scale commercial extractors compromising the amount or the purity of water that's left? And who will make that determination? Safe and clean water is a finite resource: the fact has hit us on the head throughout history, and it's going to hit us even harder—and more frequently—as the world's population grows, particularly in arid areas, as we pollute and mine more of the remaining freshwater, and as the climate heats up. Global warming will raise water and air temperatures, causing more water to evaporate, and it will affect the timing and distribution of rainfall, leading to both more flooding, in wet areas, and more drought, in dry areas.

"We are already at the limits of our resources," Peter H. Gleick, a sustainable-water-use expert and cofounder of the Pacific Institute, says. "Look at Las Vegas, look at the drought in the Southeast, the contamination of water in the Northeast," with gasoline additives, like methyl tertiary butyl ether, and other industrial chemicals. And so who controls what's left of our freshwater—locals who depend on it for survival, or corporations that sell it for profit—matters a great deal, whether that water comes from an aquifer in western Maine, or an aquifer in the Philippines, Australia, or Indonesia, where companies have already privatized either supplies or delivery systems. Dearborn may seem focused only on his backyard, but he has an intuitive understanding that his situation is representative of the struggle over the global water commons.

Waite motors to the pond's south end, collects more data, then makes his way back toward Dearborn's place. In nearly seventeen feet of water, he cautiously tugs on a tether tied to a buoy. He pulls in handful after handful of line, a worried look on his face. When a slimy gray cylinder comes to rest on the boat deck, he sighs and says, "I'm glad that was still there. That's a four-thousand-dollar piece of equipment." Every forty-five minutes for six months, the cylinder recorded six different parameters. The data would give Waite a picture of the lake's health—how it had changed over this study and, by comparing some of his data with information gleaned by a volunteer lake-monitoring program, over several years.

Back on land, Waite loads his truck with sample-filled coolers. He's about to climb into the driver's seat when Dearborn approaches and asks, "Do you want to see my well?" Hesitating for just a moment, Waite says, "Sure." Dearborn mounts his tiny tractor and trundles into the woods. Waite and I follow on foot. At the well, which sticks up about three feet and has a concrete cover, Dearborn brushes off some pine needles, hooks a chain to its handle, and raises it with a flick of a lever on his tractor.

"I dug this well myself," he says proudly. We look inside the tiled column and duly note that the water level is low. "It's been sucking air on and off for two weeks now," he says. Dearborn peers at Waite and, looking as if he'd just presented a crucial piece of evidence to a jury, purses his lips expectantly. Waite nods.

In October of 2005, Elbridge Russell was driving east out of Fryeburg on Route 302 when he stopped to rescue a turtle attempting to cross the road. He thought it looked like a Blanding's, a state-endangered species, but they'd never been recorded this far north or west. After confirming the identification with local wildlife officials, Russell returned the turtle to the roadside. It headed toward the Saco, toward safety, but suddenly one of Poland Spring's business plans was in danger. The company had requested a permit to build a truck-loading station barely a mile down the road, where springwater pumped from the adjacent town of Denmark—105 million gallons a year—would be piped several miles and then into trucks bound for bottling plants. The turtle was a hurdle: if more of them were nearby, it could halt the project. Nestlé hired an independent contractor to look into the matter, and opponents of the tanker station began to pray for reptiles with yellow-spotted black shells.

It doesn't surprise Stefan Jackson, director of the Saco River Project for the Nature Conservancy, that no further turtles were found. "They looked only where they were required to look," Jackson says: the scope of the study was too limited— perhaps by design. Hard-muscled and swarthy, Jackson prowls the cramped confines of his office—the upper floor of a small Victorian house on Fryeburg's Main Street. He pushes aside maps and publicity materials, leftovers from the Saco River Project's booth at the Fryeburg Fair. As someone interested in the sustainability of natural systems, Jackson is focused on facts: how much water can be pumped from an aquifer without impairing the wetlands and waters into which it normally discharges. As an attorney, he's interested in accountability. In the Poland Spring matter, he doesn't see enough of either.

"Poland Spring says their pumping will have no impact. That's ludicrous. Every action in this ecosystem has an impact. But is it measurable or significant? It's no impact only because of what they chose to measure. As far as I know, they did no dragonfly-population study, no sinkhole study; they didn't do broad macro-invertebrate studies. They looked at the hydrology but they didn't do environmental impact surveys." Jackson sips tea from a travel mug, long gone cold. "There are other, bigger users of the Saco's aquifers—industry, agriculture, community drinking water. The big rub, environmentally, is whether pumping for bottled water is the straw that will break the camel's back."

Humans have inhabited the Fryeburg vicinity for ten thousand years, but the area is still fairly pristine, with key species of globally rare plants and animals. "What would it be like," Jackson wonders, "if we had that yearly one hundred and fifty million gallons of water back? Would there be more Blanding's turtles, more dragonflies, more silverling, more *Scirpus longii*?" The silverling is a lovely herb with tiny flowers and needlelike leaves; the *Scirpus* an elegant bulrush. All Jackson wants is for Nestlé to show that it cares for the area beyond its short-term financial returns. "I want them to catalog what's out there, record their steps, be responsible. And if they discover it's a mistake, then to acknowledge that and step in another direction."

While Jackson talks, I devour a sandwich and try to make

sense of what he's saying. I want to know if drinking Poland Spring is like an urbanite killing and wearing a baby harp seal—that is, morally indefensible. But Jackson isn't making the distinction easy; there's just too much uncertainty. "It's very clever for Nestlé to say this is a sustainable business," he continues. "They want you to think rainfall here in Maine is from the same system where Poland Spring water ends up. They are removing water from the watershed—unlike the majority of local agriculture and home use. That water isn't coming back here. And the idea that they're taking only 'extra' water"—a point Tom Brennan raises in every interview and debate—"that cracks me up. They mean water not being extracted. There is no such thing as extra water in a floodplain—it all goes somewhere in the ecosystem and something, naturally, makes use of it."

Sarah Allen, a biologist collecting baseline data on the Wards Brook wetlands for another town-sponsored study, describes a potential cascade of effects from reduced stream flows. At the driest times of year, macro-invertebrates—creatures such as worms, crayfish, and stoneflies—could become stranded or stressed. Lose macro-invertebrates and you lose fish. "Shallow water also heats up more easily," Allen says, which affects the growth of algae and plankton—fish food. With less flow, wetland vegetation could change—upland trees could move in and create shaded areas, and exotic species would have an easier time taking root.

Nestlé Waters' greatest and most oft-cited defense is its aforementioned focus on sustainability. "Why would we hurt the resource if that's what we're selling?" goes the official line. Why would a company invest fifty-one million dollars in a bottling plant if it thought the water would last only a few years? It isn't as if Nestlé would make its money back in that time: with slim margins, profits come from volume, over the long haul. Nestlé hydrogeologists work hard to determine the maximum amount of water they can sustainably pump from an aquifer, then adjust their pumping to 75 percent of that level.

But there's one problem with this approach, critics say. Protecting aquifers—the underground bathtubs from which companies pump—doesn't necessarily protect the surrounding environment. "An aquifer may contain plenty of water, but pumping from it may harm a nearby river, stream, or wetland," Robert Glennon writes in *Water Follies*. According to the Sierra Club, Nestlé's bottling operations in the United States have already degraded lakes, harmed wetlands, and lowered water tables, and its pumping continues to pose a threat to residential and agricultural water supplies.

In coastal areas, groundwater pumping by agricultural and industrial interests has allowed salt water to creep into freshwater aquifers from the sea. Elsewhere, overpumping has pulled heavy metals and other pollutants into drinking water and washed away soil or bedrock to create sinkholes—depressions in the earth's surface sometimes big enough to engulf trucks or houses. According to the U.S. Geological Survey, more than 80 percent of the nation's identified land subsidence, or sinking, is a "consequence of our exploitation of underground water." In Massachusetts, groundwater pumping for municipal supplies converts parts of the Ipswich River, in the summertime, into a shallow canyon of mud. In eastern Michigan and in eastern Texas, commercial extraction of groundwater has dried up neighbors' drinking-water wells, and in other states, reports the *Michigan Chronicle*, a Detroit weekly, "groundwater pumping has severely diminished lakes, streams and underground aquifers used for drinking water and to irrigate farm fields."

Fish aren't fairing any better: springs deliver fresh, cold, oxygen-rich water to river headwaters—trout habitat. When there's less springwater, stream temperature rises, and fish eggs die. In New Tripoli, Pennsylvania, Nestlé withdraws up to one hundred and nine million gallons of water a year from a small mountain stream, bottling it under the Deer Park label. The withdrawals, Peter Crabb, a Penn State psychologist and member of Citizens for the Preservation of Lynn Township, says, "have devastated the stream and its plant and animal inhabitants. Where there used to be native brown trout, there are now none." In his decision to halt Nestlé's pumping from Sanctuary Springs in Mecosta County, Michigan, circuit judge Lawrence Root wrote, "I am unable to find that a specific pumping rate lower than 400 gallons per minute, or any rate to date, will reduce the effects and impacts to a level that is not harmful." (The decision to halt was stayed, and Nestlé continues to pump springwater at a reduced rate while it awaits a higher-court decision on its appeal.)

The bottled-water industry claims that water for bottling is a minute portion of total water use. And it's true: in the United States, the industry takes only 0.02 percent of the total groundwater withdrawn each year. But it takes that in the same few places, not spread out over the globe, and it moves those gallons to other watersheds, unlike the gallons pumped by a local utility, which waters a community that discharges into the same watershed. A liter of Poland Spring gulped in Pomfret, Vermont, or even Poland, Maine, isn't coming back to the trout fingerlings at the Shy Beaver hatchery.

Moreover, with the market for bottled water continuing to grow, and sources of freshwater becoming ever more precious, companies are constantly on the hunt for more of it. Nestlé is already seeking new sources in upstate New York and Massachusetts, among other states, the better to meet the demands of my friends and neighbors in the tristate area. Other bottlers are on the prowl as well.

Over the years, in towns across the country, the message from Nestlé has been the same: "There's no evidence of environmental harm." And once again, it's true: it's extremely difficult to prove without a doubt that groundwater pumping has dried up a well, river, or wetland. It's easy to blame drought, another pumper, beavers, a snowless winter, or anything at all. Wells and ponds dry up even when there's *no* commercial extraction. Adverse effects to stream systems, and their related wetlands, occur slowly and are affected by many factors. The movement of groundwater, and its exact relationship to surface water, is imperfectly known.

"If the water table goes down, Poland Spring will say, 'How do you know it's us?'" Jackson says. "It's a classic defense—you can't prove a proximate cause." In Hollis, Poland Spring drilled new wells for two homeowners; locals say they went dry, but the company says they failed for mechanical reasons. "People around here are freaked-out: there's an irrational fear that the water will be gone or contaminated," Jackson says. It doesn't help that Tom Brennan, the face of Nestlé Waters in Fryeburg, is said to be standoffish. His idea of reassuring concerned citizens is to produce additional data sets.

Jackson ignores the frequent ringing of his office and cell phones. He unscrews the top of a giant pretzel jar, apparently to eat his lunch, but can't stop talking long enough to put a single rod in his mouth. "I'm really starting to think about this whole water thing as an environmental justice issue. Nestlé is pretending they're small and local"—indeed, Poland Spring's regional identification is essential to its popularity: its slogan is "What it means to be from Maine"—"but they're indifferent to the needs of people they're affecting. It's a corporation versus individuals, real people and local communities."

What if a thorough study showed that pumping actually is sustainable, I ask. "The pumping *may* be sustainable, it *may* be ecologically fine," Jackson says in a tone of frustration, "but that doesn't necessarily make it the right thing to do. Why are they suing the town of Fryeburg over the tanker station?" (Nestlé went to court because Fryeburg's board of appeals, propelled by a group called Western Maine Residents for Rural Living, overturned the planning board's initial approval of the station.)

The case is grinding its way through the legal system, but Jackson doesn't expect the protracted chess game to end with the decision. "If they lose their permit to tanker water out of town, their lawyers will claim it's malicious and undue enforcement. They will claim the pumping is sustainable, and that no one else is being scrutinized like this. They'll gum up the process for a long time. Imagine how much time and money it will take to fight it." I did, and I immediately imagined Howard Dearborn's approaching eighty-ninth birthday. "Nestlé has been in the business of water extraction for twenty years, so they have a long head start on this. They didn't idly walk into this situation."

The citizens of Fryeburg didn't know, when they first started challenging Nestlé, that they would soon be part of a growing movement, allied with angry citizens across the nation who are standing up to corporate behemoths for control of their communities. It's an uphill struggle, because most small-town Americans aren't schooled in exercising their rights, and because their opponents, as Jackson says, have all the time and money in the world to press their individual agendas.

Through an accident of geology, Fryeburg is now paying the price for America's infatuation with bottled water. But the town isn't alone. "Everywhere there is clean freshwater, these companies are coming in," Maude Barlow, founder of the Blue Planet Project, which works to stop commodification of the world's water, and the national chairperson of the Council of Canadians, Canada's largest social movement, tells the audience at a talk in Albany, New Hampshire. She cites examples of multinational corporations attempting to privatize public water companies in the United States and in Latin America and of bottlers hurrying to stake water claims. As the resource becomes more valuable, water conflicts will become more frequent. Already, Barlow says, farmers in Indonesia are fighting each other with machetes over the allotment of water that Nestlé leaves behind. Outside Johannesburg, she continues, impoverished South Africans turned for drinking water to a polluted river after the French multinational Suez took control of the local water system and made the town pump available only to those who could pay.

But the news isn't all grim. As a half-dozen Fryeburg residents listening to Barlow's talk solemnly nod, she recounts stories of communities that rejected privatization—in Bolivia and in Uruguay, in Stockton, California, Highland Park, Michigan, and nearby Barnstead, New Hampshire, which in 2006 became the first municipal government in the United States to ban corporations from pumping water for sale elsewhere.

Fryeburg, Barlow says, "is part of the global water-justice movement."

In 2004, a team of Nestlé geologists were combing over Maine maps, looking for new sources of Poland Spring water. They were interested in thick deposits of sand and gravel, the result of ancient glaciers melting into rivers. In this "high energy" situation, fine particles rush out to sea while coarse sediments settle on the river's edge. The resulting layers are thick, they make excellent filters, and they're likely to produce the sort of water that many are willing to buy. Maine has a lot of great aquifers, but not all of them have a spring at their end, produce high volumes of high-quality water, and are reasonably close to highways that lead to major markets. When the Nestlé geologists hit what looked like pay dirt in the tiny town of Kingfield, they rolled up their maps and pulled on their boots. It was time to take a walk in the woods.

It's time for me to hit the woods too. If the argument over Fryeburg's water is an argument over sustainability, I owe it to Tom Brennan to see how Poland Spring decides that taking X amount of water will leave more than enough behind. Brennan and his team determine pumping rates based on complicated hydrogeological models built inside computers. But the data have to come from somewhere, and so on a cold March day I drive north out of Fryeburg and keep going until I'm forty miles from the Canadian border.

Just west of Kingfield, population eleven hundred, I bump down the rutted driveway of the Howe Farm and park in a snowy field. A middle-aged man in a wool cap skis out of the woods and offers me a pair of snowshoes. A consulting hydrogeologist for Nestlé, Rich Fortin has agreed to show me the company's newest springs, which will soon be providing 200 million gallons of water a year to a bottling plant rising on the south side of Kingfield. The day is overcast and cold, but tromping through the crust soon warms us. At the forest's edge, Fortin stops at a capped pipe rising a foot from the snow and drops in a line that ends with a transducer. The device is the size of a small flashlight, and it beeps when it hits the water's surface. The well is fifty-four feet deep: subtract the transducer's 6.01 feet of tether and you get the elevation of the water. Fortin records the data and we trudge on. Only sixty-nine more wells to go.

The forest here is young, mostly white cedar and hemlock, spruce and birch. The air is alive with the peeping of chickadees and the *skronk* of blue jays. Fortin leads me toward a pool of water and directs my gaze toward a boil of bark chips at its bottom, about five inches down. "That's spring number one," he says, unexcited. The water looks dark, the edges of the small pool are steep and mossy, and frozen deer tracks are all over the place. Automatically my mind flashes on the Poland Spring ads of yore, with animated Bambis prancing around a woodland

pool. I quote the ad—"from deep in the woods of Maine"—
but Fortin, who's even older than I am, has no idea what I'm
talking about. (Either that or it's a touchy subject. The slogan,
which perhaps unconsciously channeled Thoreau's *Maine Woods*,
seems to have been dropped after Nestlé settled the suit that
claimed Poland Spring water came not from deep in the woods
but from boreholes along highways. Still, the company loves to
show its springs to the media, perhaps because they're such a
strong visual antidote to the industrial facilities that bottle their
output.)

On this day, Fortin and two colleagues are collecting data
at monitoring wells and at springheads—pipes driven directly
into the springs. "The level inside will be higher than the pool
itself," Fortin explains. "This gives us an idea of the hydraulic
push behind the water." He moves downstream to a brook and
measures the water's temperature and depth in the middle of a
flume—an hourglass-shaped half-pipe placed in the streambed.
When it's running full, Fortin knows, this brook is producing
156 gallons per minute, or 224,640 gallons a day.

The identification of six springs on the Howe Farm, back in
2004, set in motion a massive (and massively expensive) effort to
quantify how much underground water is available for pumping
and how much of that can be taken without harm—a procedure
that smaller companies don't follow. Nestlé brought in hydrogeologists to survey soil and conduct seismic experiments.
Along transects, they repeatedly laid down five hundred feet
of cable, set off the four to six dynamite charges that ran its
length, and measured the resulting sound waves, which gave

them a picture of soil horizons: coarse, medium, fine, bedrock. Next, they laid down cables with electrical probes that sent shocks 120 feet into the earth. The resulting sound waves, when graphed, would indicate the soil's conductivity—that is, how rapidly water would move horizontally and vertically through the sand and gravel layers.

After mapping the solid features of the underworld, technicians drilled monitoring wells and began calculating the elevation of the water table. Researchers studied land-use maps from fifty years ago and interviewed elderly town residents and foresters. "You want to know everything you can about the land's history," Brennan says. No springwater company wants to discover its property was once a chemical dump. Lab technicians compared water samples from each spring and its borehole. Flipping through a thick binder of graphs and reports, Fortin shows me a series of Piper diagrams, which are shaped like triangles and diamonds. He says their plotted points reveal an excellent geochemical match between the water that sprang from the earth and the water that Nestlé had pumped. To label borehole water springwater, says the FDA, the two must be "substantially similar."

All this was in preparation for the big event: a seven-day pump test, in which water is extracted continuously from a larger and larger area and shunted through a pipe to the river. "You pump until you get a change, until the level in the observation well starts to stabilize," Fortin says. Such a test defines the size of the borehole recharge area; it determines how much water is available in the aquifer under the property; and it establishes that the natural springs continue to flow despite continuous pumping. "Once you see a response in the spring and the well," Brennan adds, "you keep pumping beyond that. At some point, maybe a day after, it stabilizes. This way you can estimate what operational pumping would be. If you pump at a steady state, you won't be drawing on surface water."

For months after the pump test, the hydrologic team will continue to measure stream depth and flow rates, plugging real numbers into their computer model. In theory, the more numbers that go in, the stronger the model. But still, a model isn't reality. No hydrogeologist can say with absolute certainty what this magnitude of extraction will mean for the environment years or even decades into the future. (And attorneys don't like to take cases that depend on proof ten years down the road.) The literature of hydrogeologic modeling is peppered with such words as *optimization*, *probabilistic*, and *conceptual*. And the history of dried-up springs and salt water seeping into sweet water is littered with models that predicted adequate flow.

"Modelers always argue with each other, they talk about 'trends' and 'possibilities' because no one can actually see it," Stefan Jackson says. "They say there's four hundred million gallons of headroom in the aquifer, but however well formulated, it's only an assumption."

"Some hydrogeologists will say whatever they're paid to say," Robert Glennon, speaking generally of the field, tells me later. "I call them hydrostitutes."

I spend another hour with Fortin in the woods. It's pleasant work in a pleasant place: 160 acres of forest and field, home to deer and turkeys, coyotes and bobcats. Out here in the fresh air, there is no hint of the strife behind the permitting process or the high-emotional battles that have accompanied other new operations, either in Maine or across the country. The stakes are high: already Nestlé is pumping water from Pierce Pond township, about twenty-three miles north of here, and from Dallas Plantation, thirty miles west. Both sources will feed water to the Kingfield plant.

"It would make more sense to tanker the water to Hollis than bottle it here," Brennan tells me at the plant site, where bulldozers roar in the background. So why build here? I ask. "Because there's so much controversy over these water-development projects. If we want a tanker loading station with one hundred trucks, and we don't leave any economic benefit behind—any jobs, any health insurance—it's gonna be an unpleasant experience." It already *is* unpleasant, over in Fryeburg. "To do it a second time, it's gonna be even more unpleasant," Brennan continues. "So we wanted a bottling plant somewhere in this region."

Brennan had invited me to Kingfield to see how scientists determine sustainability. It was similar, in a way, to the reason I had visited Miles Waite, who, by measuring and sampling Lovewell Pond, is trying to determine if Howard Dearborn's claim—that the pumping is unsustainable—is true. But Brennan also wanted me to get a feel for a community that, after sober examination of the pros and cons, decided to welcome the company. When Kim Jeffery, the CEO of Nestlé Waters North America, announced it would build a plant in Kingfield, he said, "It has taken a couple of years, but that is how trust is built. When you have a project that takes an extended period of time, where expectations are met and people do what they say they will do, then you have a very strong foundation." Brennan echoes that sentiment when he tells me, "Kingfield is a great example of a community that took a sensible and comprehensive approach to economic development."

Fryeburg, of course, is just the opposite.

Chapter 4

THE CRADLE OF THE SACO

THE FRYEBURG WATER Company has supplied the village of Fryeburg since 1883, at first from brooks that spill down a small mountain north of town, and then from a spring that bubbles in the woods between Portland Street and Lovewell Pond. "I put in a perforated pipe that led to a baffle pipe that went into a pot," Hugh Hastings, president of the water company, tells me when I stop in to get his side of the story after I'd visited Howard Dearborn. The system was a bit crude, but it worked from 1955 to 1995.

Hastings is eighty years old, with a crevassed face and slicked-back silvered hair. Wearing a dark Windbreaker, he sits behind a cluttered desk in a small storefront—the water company headquarters. Gold wall-to-wall carpeting and venetian blinds give the office a dusty sepia aspect, and family photos decorate the plywood walls. If the decor is meant to imply no one is making a killing by selling water, it succeeds royally.

Privately owned, the Fryeburg Water Company has been in the hands of a few local families since its founding and currently has thirty-three shareholders. Roughly half of them are

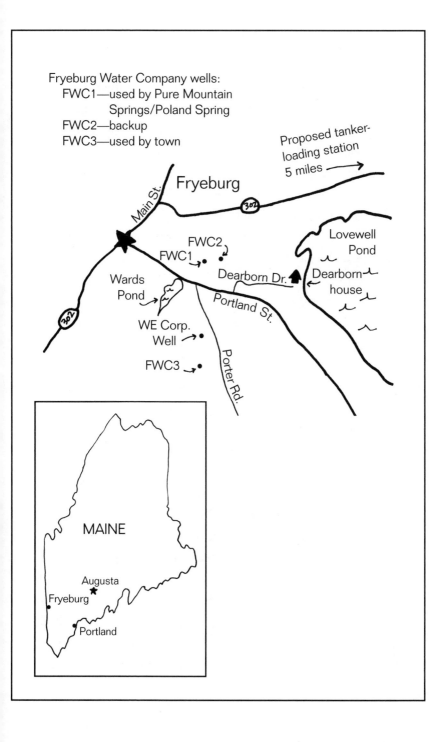

related to the Hastings family, and Hugh's son John, the company's superintendent, holds the most shares. In itself, the ownership arrangement isn't unusual: private water companies were the norm in the United States throughout the nineteenth century, but as cities grew and health issues intensified, local governments stepped in. According to the National Association of Water Companies, the proportion of water services in the United States provided by private companies—whether measured by customers served or volume of water handled—has remained close to 15 percent since World War II.

I glance around the room and note, taped to a filing cabinet across the room, a Ben Franklin quote: "When the well runs dry, we shall know the value of water." In fact, Fryeburg's well *did* run dry a few years previously, and since then the townsfolk have learned more than they ever wanted about the value of the stuff that bubbles from their stratified soils. It all started back in 1995, when the state told Hastings that, due to new drinking-water regulations, he could no longer collect water from that baffle pipe and pot. The company could either build an expensive filtration system, or it could dig a borehole. Hastings called in a hydrogeologist named Eric Carlson, who worked at a fancy-pants engineering firm in Portland.

Over the years he'd been working in Maine, Carlson told me earlier, he'd "learned where all the water was." He'd seen the water trucks rolling through the state, and he had a pretty good sense of water quality in this area. Carlson has blue eyes that twinkle over high cheekbones, wavy, graying hair, and teeth so evenly gapped they look as if they've been machined. Together with Hastings, in 1995, Carlson had walked into the woods off

Portland Street to take a look at the water company's spring site. "Hugh said the soil around here would be all clay," Carlson said. "He got out his excavator and he started to dig some holes." And what did he find? "Lots of sand." Sand was good: sand was a filter. The water kept bubbling up, and at a rate that told Carlson there was more than enough for the town. "That's when I had an idea," he said. "Why not start a facility and sell bulk water?" He turned to Hastings and said, "Let's go into business."

Carlson built borehole number one for the Fryeburg Water Company, as he'd been contracted to do. Then, after Hastings got permission to travel through Howard Dearborn's woods, Carlson dug borehole number two as a backup, not far from the first. Then, with his new partner, John Hastings (Hugh's son, that is), he formed a company called Pure Mountain Springs and started purchasing tankerloads of water, at regular town rates (less than a penny a gallon), from the Fryeburg Water Company. Pure Mountain Springs then turned around and sold that water, at four cents more per gallon, to Poland Spring. The operation started small, taking just eight million gallons a year. And then it grew.

But no one knew quite how large Pure Mountain had become until January of 2004, when the borehole that serves town customers, number one, quit pumping. Hugh Hastings says it was a mechanical problem that left villagers dry for more than a day, and with low pressure that necessitated boiling water for four more. Meanwhile, the tanker trucks kept filling up with Fryeburg water and rolling out to Poland Spring bottling plants. When the town's pump came back on, Pure Mountain

Springs was suddenly taking water from Fryeburg's original spring well, number one, and the town was drinking from a *third* well recently built by Eric Carlson and John Hastings, across the street and up Porter Road. (The town could also use well number two.) The whole thing seemed a bit off to me: public utility commissions generally must approve switches in source water, but no approval marked the swap from well one to well three, and the Fryeburg Water Company hadn't alerted its customers to the change. Why was it so important for Pure Mountain to use well one? Because it had received all its operating permits based on the water quality of the original spring.

Months passed, and a citizens group announced the results of a twenty-four-hour truck count: nearly a hundred tankers, each capable of holding 8,440 gallons, were pulling out of Fryeburg every day. Was that a lot of water? Compared to what the town used—about 200,000 gallons per day in the summer, half that in winter—yes. Did the town have any say about it? No. As a regular customer of the Fryeburg Water Company, Pure Mountain Springs can buy all the water it wants—no cap or permit needed. The moment residents realized how much water was leaving town, and who was profiting, was the moment their faith in the Fryeburg Water Company—and in one of the town's most prominent families—began to waver.

Trying to figure out who is taking water from where in Fryeburg confounds me, and plenty of others. "There's no getting to the bottom of it," Jim Wilfong, a former state legislator who started a group called H2O for ME to protect Maine aquifers, says. The Fryeburg Water Company doesn't make a lot of money, but its assets—the springs and land—are thought to be worth tens of millions. Between 2003 and 2007, Pure Mountain Springs had revenue of roughly three million dollars, from which it paid the Fryeburg Water Company roughly eight hundred thousand dollars. To its credit, the town is currently trying to regulate future pumping in Wards Brook, but when the planning board holds "informational" meetings, residents leave as mystified as when they arrived. "I think the planning board chairman sidesteps questions," Emily Fletcher, the town librarian, says. "People *hear* what he says, but they don't know *what* he says."

"It would be easy to understand if you could see it," Wilfong says. "But this is all purposefully hidden. It's easy to move around if people don't know what's cooking. It's the same all around the world." I think about the way New York City bullied landowners in the Catskill and Delaware watersheds into selling their property, how Los Angeles outwitted desperate valley farmers to appropriate the Owens River, how Chicago strongmen reversed the flow of the Chicago River to shunt their city's sewage all the way to St. Louis. Sneaking water around might seem difficult, but it isn't always: wells are dispersed, no one can see how much of it moves through pipes and into tankers, and no one knows for sure how much remains underground.

When I ask Hugh Hastings how much water Pure Mountain Springs and the water company itself pump from Wards Brook, he throws a lot of numbers at me, interchanging cubic feet and gallons, and gallons per day and gallons per year. He punches numbers into an adding machine as he talks, and I admit to him

I have a hard time keeping Poland Spring and Pure Mountain Springs straight. He says genially, "I mix 'em up too!" Essentially, they are the same.

But Hastings sticks to his story: "All of this was done with good intentions, for the people of Fryeburg." The income to the Fryeburg Water Company from Pure Mountain—$222,493 in 2006—"subsidizes" town rates, he says: it keeps them low and finances maintenance of town pipes. In other words, John Hastings and Eric Carlson aren't just running a tidy business: they're helping the community. "Most people don't understand that," Hastings continues. "They're worried about trucks and the town going dry. I see no sign of it. But some people on the pond have a lot of pull—they talk."

"Howard Dearborn says his well is dry," I say.

"Maybe he pulled his pump up," Hastings says.

The phone rings, and the president of the water company mollifies a customer without water. "He put in his pipe wrong," he says to me. "It's always freezing." Then he gets back to the pond. "I think this is sustainable, and I think Lovewell is fine. I'm an environmentalist, but I'm a realist. I believe in cutting timber. No one complains about trucks hauling wood or mills making money." Lumber trucks don't haul twenty-four hours a day, of course, and not year-round. "The water is just like air here," Hastings continues. "When you pump and it's still bubbling up on top, there's still plenty. Yes, we're taking it away, but the brook hasn't changed how it looks."

After leaving Hastings, I drive a short distance down Portland Street, park opposite the pumping station, and watch empty tanker trucks pull in and, twenty minutes later, pull out—loaded for plants in either Poland or Hollis. I try to make sense of what's going on here. I realize the town is small, and its political and family dynamics unusually tense. But it isn't normal for a private water company to sell unlimited quantities of water to a shareholder (John Hastings, that is) who then flips it to the largest food company in the world. It's unusual, to say the least, that the lawyer hired to negotiate the deal with Pure Mountain Springs is Peter Hastings, Hugh's brother, and that Pure Mountain Springs operates without a permit from the town. Sure, some of the income from that company goes toward maintenance, but it seems to me a hell of a conflict of interest. Even more galling is that townspeople have absolutely nothing to say about it. So many of the deals were made without public scrutiny.

I contemplate Fryeburg's inch-by-inch struggle to curb Poland Spring: two different moratoriums (one on new water-pumping operations and another, recently proposed, on new water-trucking operations), the approval and then denial of the tanker station permit, the prospect of a new water ordinance that will keep any new pumpers from drilling into the Wards Brook aquifer. The proposed rule sounds protective to me, but Dearborn swears it would set in stone the pumping of current operators—Pure Mountain Springs, the Fryeburg Water Company, and the WE Corporation (Jeff Walker and Rick Eastman's setup on Porter Road), which are already, he says, taking way too much.

Jim Wilfong, a former assistant administrator for international trade at the Small Business Administration under the

Clinton administration, offered me some perspective when I phoned him later on. "This is what a water war looks like," he said. The endless meetings, the legal challenges, the tiny changes in rules. He linked Fryeburg's troubles to privatization issues on a global scale. "The question is, are we going to be involved in this discussion or do we leave it up to a multinational corporation? We won't understand Nestlé's full intent until it's too late: do they want our water just for bottles? Here in the U.S., not just in Fryeburg, we're seeing how difficult it is for citizens to look after their rights, to say, 'This is how we want our community to look.' Once we sign up with Nestlé, there's no way out."

I wait for a water truck to finish its turn onto Portland Street, then head south to visit the cofounder of Pure Mountain Springs. We meet in Eric Carlson's Woodard & Curran office, in Portland, because the hydrogeologist isn't particularly welcome in Fryeburg. He says the hostility there has taken him completely by surprise.

"It's the age-old question," Carlson says. "Whose water is it? Well, it's your right to take it from your property in Maine. I've been getting all this flack. People are more emotional about water than trees or gravel or lobster in the ocean. And it's free! But it's not any different from timber or oil. People don't understand this pumping won't affect the ecosystem. Why don't they complain about the profits of a gravel pit? The owner just digs a hole in the ground and sells it for ten dollars a yard."

After drilling well number two, Carlson and Hastings bought five acres of land along Porter Road, uphill from wells one and two. The road starts off paved but quickly turns to dirt as it runs between Wards Brook Pond and a tree nursery on the right, and a collection of abandoned industrial buildings on the left. It continues for miles, up past a gravel pit, a former town dump, two kettle-hole ponds, and forty acres owned by the Nature Conservancy, and behind a tiny regional airport. "I bought the land to protect the basin," Carlson explains—the town had planned to build a heavy-equipment garage on the plot, and he didn't want his well contaminated with runoff.

Carlson and Hastings then bought another nine acres up Porter Road and drilled a third borehole. "I own it, but the town uses it for free," he says. Why? "I didn't want the water from Pure Mountain Springs and the Fryeburg Water Company to come from one spot. The water company puts fluoride and chlorine into its pipes—I didn't want to risk cross-contamination."

Soon, Pure Mountain would buy another twenty-six-acre parcel up Porter Road.

"For a well?" I ask, wincing at the thought of further complications.

"I *am* thinking about drilling another well," Carlson says, "but I'd have to go through the permitting process." He lets that thought hang, then moves to a whiteboard. He starts to draw a graph. *Power* is on the vertical axis and *interest* on the horizontal. He draws a point far to the right and low. "It is a sociopolitical nightmare to have someone with lots of interest and no power," he says heatedly. "They can create a huge amount of problems. So it's very important to engage those people—to help them understand." It's a funny spin, I think, on Margaret Mead's pronouncement: "Never doubt that a small group of thoughtful, committed citizens can change the world. Indeed, it is the only thing that ever has." An empowered minority, I'm guessing, is the last thing in the world Carlson wants to see.

Before I leave Woodard & Curran, which counts Nestlé Waters among its clients, I ask Carlson if he'll show me the springs of Fryeburg, over which so much bad blood has spilled. Hugh Hastings had turned down my request, and the spring property is fenced and monitored, so naturally I feel compelled to get in. Carlson says he can't, but John Hastings will.

I wait in the driveway of a weathered farmhouse near Fryeburg center until a pickup rolls up. The driver lowers his tinted window a few inches and tells me to get in. I sit down next to a large man with calloused hands and no time for formalities. A pipe fitting rolls across the seat as we ride over to the Poland Spring tanker station, no seat belts, through a locked gate and downhill to a small pool of water.

When the truck stops near a wellhead building—the same stone-walled-and-green-roofed design I'd seen in Hollis—Hastings points at a kidney-shaped pool of water. "Well number one," he says, also known as Evergreen Spring on the Poland Spring label. The pool has cemented stone walls, and Hastings makes sure I notice the sand bubbling up from its bottom—just as Rich Fortin had in Kingfield. There's some aquatic growth down there too, and a bloom of rust on some sunken stones. According to papers filed by attorney Tom

Sobol with the Connecticut Superior Court in June of 2003—in a class-action suit accusing Poland Spring of false advertising—this pool is not natural but a man-made formation, dug below the water table. "It's a spring," Hastings says sternly when I ask. It isn't "deep in the woods of Maine," like the Hollis spring, but at least you can't see the road from here. (The suit was settled out of court in 2004.)

We take a quick peek at well number two, just downhill, then drive back up to the loading station. Within seconds, a tanker driver pulls in, parks his truck on the cement pad, and pulls a hose from a long steel box. He snaps on purple latex gloves, opens a box at the back of the tanker, squirts alcohol on a coupling, and plugs the hose into his truck. With the flick of a switch, Wards Brook water races in, sounding like heavy rain on a metal roof. After a twenty-minute downpour, the driver unhitches the hose and drives off in a pneumatic whoosh. Within seconds, another tanker starts to fill.

"They just keep coming," I say to Hastings, but he's uninterested in discussing the sustainability of the aquifer, or much of anything. "I'm not a talker," he says. When I ask why Howard Dearborn's well might have gone dry, Hastings says it was a loose nut on a valve stem, now fixed.

I think Hastings is done with me, but he wants to show me well number three, up Porter Road and down a rutted drive. I see the stone house in the woods, and then suddenly I'm being tossed from side to side on the slippery seat. We're driving through the forest in a couple of feet of wet snow. "There's a spring," Hastings says, pointing to a monitoring pipe sticking three feet out of the ground. Water squirts up in a thin plume.

"There's another." He's pretty low-key about these fountains in the forest. I wonder how far and why we are driving into the woods. When the truck gets stuck, he says, "I guess you can get out. There's the spring for well number three." Later, I'll wonder if Hastings had misspoken. According to Bill Black, Maine's deputy public advocate, this water isn't technically springwater. If it were, he says, Pure Mountain Springs would be selling *that* water to Nestlé, instead of leasing the well to the town.

"Can I taste it?" I ask.

"Sure," Hastings says. He stays near the truck while I walk ahead. Stepping onto the slimy circle of concrete that rings the central pipe, I lean in and sip. Yum. I'm getting used to this stuff.

Maybe the issue in Fryeburg isn't the aquatic environment; maybe Howard Dearborn is wrong about the cause of Lovewell Pond's decline. That still leaves the truck traffic and truck pollution to argue with, and it still leaves the issue of economic fairness. How much is Nestlé giving back to Maine citizens who've done so much to protect the state's waters—by regulating industry, investing in public sewer systems, cleaning up oil and gasoline spills, buying land for conservation, and requiring setbacks for development along waterways, among other initiatives? And how can the company be stopped from taking even more? Jim Wilfong is a realist: he knows he can't run Poland Spring out of town, so he's come up with another scheme. He and his group H2O for ME are asking the state to levy a per gallon fee on "nontraditional" users of water. The bottled-water tax would fund a Fresh Water Resource Board to monitor and protect water supplies from overwithdrawal.

I meet Wilfong, fifty-nine, at the Jockey Cap, where a steady stream of customers comes in for coffee, a copy of the *Conway Daily Sun*, and gasoline. Wilfong knows, and greets, everyone. He teaches business management at the University of Southern Maine, and he lives—and farms Christmas trees—in Stow, just north of Fryeburg.

We grab our own coffees and newspapers; then Wilfong and I drive north out of town along the Saco River, past swaths of golden farm fields. Fryeburg may lack the polish of nearby communities, but it is rich in natural beauty: streaked with water and ringed by glacier-carved mountains and hills. Not half a mile from the town's single traffic light, the farmhouses look honest and plain. Wilfong points out the old course of the Saco, which—way back before state and federal laws prohibited the wholesale manipulation of vast landscapes—farmers ditched, diked, and rerouted to create some of the county's richest farmland (and to shorten the trip downstream to the coast).

We look west, over the floodplain, toward New Hampshire's Crawford Notch, the source of the Saco. The river drains eight hundred thousand acres of White Mountain National Forest before crossing into the state of Maine, and it floods—sometimes rising fifteen feet—every spring. The runoff forms New England's largest intact floodplain ecosystem, and it's responsible, in part, for the region's great diversity of flora and fauna, including its agricultural bounty. Rainwater percolates slowly through the region's fine glacial soils and returns to streams and springs purified: the Saco receives the state's highest ranking for water quality. More than one hundred thousand people drink groundwater from its floodplain; from its headwaters in the mountains to its outlet in the Atlantic Ocean, the river slakes the thirst of a quarter million people.

To the Sokokis Indians, Fryeburg's first settlers, the Saco was "the mythic pathway to the White Mountains, home of the sacred spirits." Today, this pathway is under enormous pressure from residential and commercial development along its length. The more water pumped from aquifers and streams that feed the Saco, the less clean water ends up in the river, and the more impurities are concentrated. The same scenario plays out across the country: nearly 40 percent of the nation's rivers and streams are too polluted for fishing and swimming, to say nothing of drinking.

"I'm a person who sees patterns," Wilfong says as he drives. "I looked at this water issue and I saw big trends. It takes one thousand tons of water to grow one ton of grain. If you control water, you control food. These issues are environmental, they're economic, and they're legal." They are local too: as the West continues to dry out, agricultural production could shift to the East, where crops don't require irrigation. Fryeburg has plenty of open farmland.

Wilfong points southeast, over the tree line. "See that rise of land? On the other side of it is Denmark. It's full of ponds. If Poland Spring builds a plant in town to bottle water from Fryeburg and Denmark, we're going to have seven hundred and fifty thousand extra vehicle trips—including water trucks and employees and service vehicles—a year in town."

We head down Cornshop Road, past the buildings where

Burnham & Morrill once canned Fryeburg's corn, then turn south, past the Fryeburg Fairgrounds, and into town. "But where would a bottling plant go?" I ask. I had heard that Nestlé had approached two landowners in town, offering them one million dollars apiece just to negotiate. The talks went nowhere, which angered some residents eager for jobs.

"Maybe the old Bailey Manufacturing plant," Wilfong says.

"Where's that?" I ask, just as we turn onto Porter Road.

"Here," Wilfong says, pointing to an abandoned factory on our left. "Bailey made lumber here, which they trucked to Pennsylvania to be made into furniture. Then the company went bankrupt, and that's when Nestlé came in." I'm having trouble imaging this industrial area—with its derelict buildings and mothballed trucks—transformed into a showplace like the Hollis plant. It's easier to picture kids guzzling beer out here than deer nuzzling around mossy springs. But Fryeburg, for all its out-of-season torpor, once bustled with economic activity: sawmills and timber operations, a shoe manufacturing plant, a couple of machine shops, corn shops, and dozens of thriving dairy farms. Now, it has the water-extraction business, which contributes nothing to the town's long-term economic welfare (though it does enrich the privately owned water company).

Naturally, Poland Spring isn't wild about the idea of a bottled-water tax. "Wilfong has this idea that taxing our business because it's growing is going to be the salvation of the state's economics," Tom Brennan had said when we met at the Hollis plant. In 2005, Wilfong had proposed taxing Poland Spring twenty cents for each gallon of water withdrawn from the state, to be put into a public trust for economic development. The proposal didn't succeed, but now Wilfong is calling for a new tax, of an unspecified amount he characterized as "considerably less."

"The economics of a tax just don't work," Brennan had said, "because our competition is Coke and Pepsi, and they bottle their water in their areas of distribution. We're transporting water from northwestern Maine; if you tax that, we're just not competitive. We won't build up there."

He insisted that the margins on Poland Spring were "very, very thin." (In 2006, Nestlé's 32 percent share of the U.S. bottled-water market—of which Poland Spring is by far the biggest moneymaker—brought profits of $7.46 billion.) "Nestlé has seven regional brands," Brennan continued. "If the tax were implemented, it would not make sense to expand the business into Maine. It would make sense to move somewhere else."

"Hogwash!" Stefan Jackson blurts when I ask if such a thing is likely. "They're not going to leave. Poland Spring is in Fryeburg, on Wards Brook, because forty percent of what comes out of the aquifer comes back in a year. They're not going to leave because the hydrogeology and the way the watershed has been managed make this one of the greatest springwater sources in the United States. That water is very pure."

In a television debate between Wilfong and Brennan, the moderator asked Brennan if he thought consumers would pay a higher price for springwater if they knew part of the price, the tax, was going toward environmental preservation, sort of like Ben & Jerry's "one percent for peace" or the Rainforest Alliance's certified-sustainable chocolate. Visibly agitated, Brennan changed the subject. "Coke and Pepsi aren't taxed," he said.

Wilfong reminded Brennan that Maine's public and private sectors had spent billions to keep the state's water clean: Poland Spring traded on Maine's pristine image but paid little for the water it extracted. Brennan reminded Wilfong that Poland Spring had a payroll of $37 million a year and employed six hundred people statewide (since the debate the numbers have risen to $46 million and seven hundred employees). It's the same defense used by any beleaguered manufacturer: changes will cost us money, we'll be forced to lay off workers, and higher prices will deprive consumers of a product they might want to buy.

Watching them spar, I feel for Brennan. He's a nice guy, overworked, and a bit out of his element. But why *should* he be any good at corporate communications? He is a scientist, after all, not a professional pacifier. Not only is he called upon to gather and interpret hydrogeological data, and to pursue permits to drill wells, build infrastructure, and withdraw and transport water, but he must also respond to turtle alerts and field media inquiries, and defend Nestlé in print and in person. The job is only getting tougher as the company grows more successful and opponents of water privatization more emboldened. Against the ropes, Nestlé has organized focus groups and hired the conservative pollster Frank Luntz, among other consultants, to help share—and spin—its message.

Ever since the scope of Nestlé's activities in Fryeburg became generally known, in 2004, local residents have been trying to get a grip on what may be both a blessing and a curse. The town has collected information on its aquifer, the better to understand its resilience and potential, and it has held listening sessions, meetings, and hearings—some of them excruciating with details—to tackle the seemingly endless legal issues that crop up when others want what you've got. Now, two days before Fryeburg's annual town meeting, Jim Wilfong gathers half a dozen Nestlé opponents in Howard Dearborn's office to discuss an ordinance that, if approved by voters, would exclude new pumpers from Wards Brook and, according to this group, hand Nestlé a virtual monopoly on the aquifer's water.

"You've got to feel the room, don't lose your audience," Wilfong advises those who plan to speak against the ordinance. "Hannah, you've got to say just one thing, bite your tongue, and sit down." Hannah Warren, who is short and energetic, with a red bob, has been fighting Poland Spring with Wilfong for forty months. A native of Fryeburg, with family roots that go back to the town's founding, Warren spent years working as an accountant for PricewaterhouseCoopers in New York and other cities before returning home ten years ago. Quick to react and sharp-tongued, Warren takes no offense at Wilfong's remark: she knows the very sound of her voice, to say nothing of its volume, annoys Gene Bergoffen, the head of the planning board. She seems to like that.

"Emily Fletcher should go last," Wilfong says. Fletcher is sixty years old, the town librarian. "She has credibility, and people will listen to her." Heads nod.

The group agrees to steer clear of ad hominem attacks and

state simply that the proposed ordinance is flawed: the document is eighteen pages long, it's been posted on the town Web site for only four days, it refers to a section that doesn't actually appear in any of its pages. In short, no one understands it. What's more, the town's most recent aquifer study hasn't been completed.

"Here is proof they don't have all the information," Dearborn says, sounding frail. He's sitting apart from the group in an upholstered chair, holding aloft the study he commissioned from Miles Waite. Dearborn has had the results for more than a month but he hasn't revealed them; he's milking this moment for all it's worth. "The study proves that pumping hurts the pond," he says. "I'm going to hold it up at the meeting to show they don't have all the information." But what does the study say, exactly? Dearborn shakes his head and says, with finality, "Not until after the vote." The group looks perplexed.

"What if the ordinance passes?" someone asks.

"Then I'll sue them for voting without this knowledge. I want to show, first, that they're corrupt, and then show who is pushing this decision without complete information."

After the meeting, Dearborn wants to show me his pump. As we walk downstairs, I ask if he had a loose nut on a valve stem, as John Hastings had said.

"I fixed that, but it's still sucking air." Dearborn had built the vacuum pump in his basement to remove radon from his well water; now he uses it to take out air. He throws a switch, the plastic cylinder fills with bubbly water, swirls clockwise, then settles when Dearborn turns off the pump. Ordinarily, the tank vents itself. Now, Dearborn needs to sit and watch the contraption until it cavitates; then he shuts the pump off until the well recuperates, then pumps again, repeating until his water tank has sufficient pressure. "Normally you don't see any air in the cylinder," he says. "Ten years ago, I had no problem with my water." He gives me the same expectant look he'd given Miles Waite, out at the well in the woods.

"I've studied engineering all my life," Dearborn says. "I had one year of college and was employing twenty-five people by the time I was twenty-four." To start his own machining business, which he called the Howard Manufacturing Company, in Berea, Ohio, he'd borrowed fourteen hundred dollars. He eventually renamed this company Dearborn, Inc., and in the early 1960s, founded Dearborn Precision Tubular Products in Fryeburg, where he'd visited on vacations. The company is now the largest employer in town.

We're back upstairs now, where every electrical outlet and light switch is labeled with an alphanumeric, and Dearborn shows me his entry in a who's who of engineers, finishing up with "So I *do* know something of what I'm talking about, Mr. Bergoffen!" In Dearborn's personal cosmology it is essential to make the connection between air in his pump and Poland Spring's activities in the Wards Brook aquifer. And to do that he needs to remind the world of his credentials. Though he'd built his own well and his own pump, to say nothing of components for tanks, space vehicles, medical equipment, deepwater drilling rigs, and nuclear submarines and reactors, there are still those who think Dearborn is not only cantankerous but a kook, and his well dry due to mechanical error—his. The very idea outrages Dearborn, perhaps even more than the suggestion that Lovewell Pond has milfoil.

Chapter 5

THE PUBLIC TROUGH

WAY BACK WHEN I first contracted water on the brain, probably from the good people of Fryeburg, I started a poll: do you know where your tap water comes from? Most people, even those who knew exactly how many miles the arugula on their plate had traveled, had no idea. Back in the day, everyone knew the source of his or her drinking water: its purity was a matter of life and death. Today, there is an infrastructure disconnect: we don't know how water gets into our homes, where our energy comes from, or where our wastewater goes once it swirls down the drain. Not only can't most of the respondents I poll name the source of their water, they don't know whether it is surface or groundwater.

Groundwater would be the safer guess—that's what a slight majority of Americans drink. It falls from the sky as snow or rain, then trickles through layers of organic and then inorganic material into the water table. Pumps pull the water up and store it in tanks, to be delivered by gravity or electricity, via more pumps, into homes. The rest of us drink surface water, which is pulled through intake pipes from lakes and rivers. Whether groundwater or surface water, almost all municipal supplies are dosed with a disinfectant such as chlorine (including Fryeburg's), filtered, and then piped into homes, offices, and institutions.

I live in New York City, which has the largest drinking-water system of any city in the nation. We drink surface water here, but we don't drink very locally (apologies to the locavores of Gotham). The Hudson and the East Rivers, which surround us, are salty and dirty, and we polluted and then paved our springs and streams long ago. When most New Yorkers fill a glass today, they drink what fell as rain or snow in the Catskill Mountains, west of the Hudson River and more than a hundred miles away.

"It takes about a year for a drop of rain to make its way through the system to your tap," Emily Lloyd, the commissioner of the Department of Environmental Protection (DEP), tells me on a blustery winter day, a few months after my first visit to Hollis and Fryeburg. We'd been talking about the system for hours, in a top-secret control room in a tiny upstate town, a community that seems nearly deserted except for the comings and goings of water department trucks. In a windowless room, the commissioner and a young engineer explain how they manage the city's most valuable resource while I stare at blue and green maps of the watershed, which with their ballooning reservoirs and thin connecting tubes remind me of a ruminant's alimentary canal. The system's vital statistics are huge and unreal to me—the capacity of the six largest reservoirs, the lengths of the aqueducts and tunnels—and so it is a relief to eventually burst into the brightness of the day and follow the babbling Esopus Creek down to the vast Ashokan.

We park on a bridge at the edge of the enormous reservoir and, ignoring the bluish mountains that form its backdrop and a phalanx of security guards in our foreground, gaze down onto the spillway, which curves and drops like a wedding cake, in four tiers, before sending its excess flow through a granite passage. The water that ruffles over the edge looks icy and pure. The setting is grand, just what you'd expect of an enormous public work, a massive manipulation of nature for the benefit of man. (Or at least the eight million privileged residents of New York City. The descendants of the thousands who were displaced when the reservoir drowned their homes, farms, and businesses weren't nearly so admiring, nor were the families of the hundreds of men who'd been killed while blasting, digging, and hauling rock and earth to build the thing.)

If the Ashokan Reservoir is not the one true source of the city's drinking water, akin to Perrier's Vergèze or the original Poland Spring, it is still evocative shorthand for the sprawling upstate waterworks imagined by city fathers more than a century ago, an engineering achievement on par with the Panama Canal, delivering 1.2 billion gallons of water a day through 300 miles of tunnels and aqueducts and 6,200 miles of distribution mains. Not only is this the largest drinking-water system in the country, but its product, according to city and state officials, professional taste-meisters, and native boosters, is one of the most delectable in the civilized world.

The purity of New York's tap water borders on myth. It's the envy of the nation, and it's touted in foreign-language guidebooks. Some city bakers credit its mineral content and taste for their culinary success; the stuff has been airlifted to the

Smithsonian Institution for an exhibit on New York bagel-making. The upstate water is of such good quality, and the watershed so well protected, that the Environmental Protection Agency, in charge of tap water, doesn't require the city to filter it—a distinction shared with only four other major U.S. cities: Boston, San Francisco, Seattle, and Portland, Oregon. New Yorkers drink their Esopus Creek, their Schoharie, Delaware, and Neversink rivers straight from the city's many reservoirs, with only a rough screening and, for most of the year, a shot of chlorine, to kill bacteria, with chasers of fluoride (to protect teeth), orthophosphate (to coat pipes so that metal doesn't leach into the water), and sodium hydroxide (to adjust its pH).

New York City's water wasn't always tasty, or abundant. When the Dutch arrived on the southern tip of Manhattan Island four centuries ago, they drank from the same creeks and springs as the Algonquin Indians who preceded them. But as the colony grew, residents and their animals fouled the local surface water, and intrepid water purveyors scouted farther north for new sources. Wealthier inhabitants dug private wells, but the water they produced was brackish and hard. During the Dutch period, freshwater was used for livestock and cooking: the preferred beverage was beer, which everyone, including children, drank warm.

In 1666 the new English governor of New York dug the city's first public well, but the water, distributed through wooden mains, was briny. Wells would provide some water for the next two centuries, though most of the colony drank from the area's single major source of freshwater, the Collect. Surrounded by wooded hills, this spring-fed pond covered seventy acres between

Chambers and Canal Streets, just east of the path that would become Broadway. As the colony grew, the once-beautiful Collect became a dumping ground for chamber pots, the carcasses of animals, and the effluent of tanneries and slaughterhouses. Disgusted authorities eventually filled the pond and its wetlands with earth, then built a neighborhood called Paradise Square atop the site. Alas, the high water table soon caused Paradise to sink, then stink. Affluent residents left, and Paradise Square became the notorious Five Points, a filthy neighborhood of thieves and gangs. At the turn of the century the slum was cleared, municipal buildings went up, and now all that's left to remind today's New Yorkers of this seminal spot in their city's drinking-water history is a forlorn rhombus of asphalt marked with a plaque and a small sign: COLLECT POND PARK.

As New York expanded through the nineteenth century, it had even less drinkable water. Wells were contaminated, and an increase in buildings and paved streets kept rainwater from recharging aquifers. The technology to dig deeper wells, into fresher water, didn't yet exist. Outbreaks of cholera and yellow and typhoid fever were common, as were fires that burned out of control for lack of water and pressure. Residents clamored for a solution; ignorant of the link between illness and the city's water, cholera-stricken patients pleaded, "Cold water, give us cold water!"

But demand did not produce supply. City planners had for decades scouted and squabbled over alternative sources of water and who would pay for its delivery, looking as far north as Lake George in the Adirondacks and the Housatonic River in Connecticut. In 1799, the state legislature empowered Aaron Burr's

Manhattan Company to build a water delivery system. Burr was expected to tap the Bronx River but instead pursued something much cheaper: he drilled new wells into the vile Collect. Over thirty-two years, the Manhattan Company laid a total of just twenty-three miles of pipe. Burr used surplus funds from his two-million-dollar capitalization not to water a thirsty city but to establish a bank, known today as JPMorgan Chase.

It took until the late 1820s for exasperated officials to commit to impounding the waters of the Croton River, in Westchester County, and sending ninety million gallons a day through an enormous aqueduct to distribution reservoirs in Manhattan. On October 14, 1842, the city officially opened the Croton waterworks with parades, a thirty-eight-gun salute, and speeches by ex-presidents. The New York Sacred Music Society sang "The Croton Ode," and a clear stream of Croton water spurted fifty feet from a fountain in City Hall Park. The festivities lasted for days. In the background, officials were already discussing Manhattan's need for more water.

From that point on, the water system grew just as New York did. By 1890, engineers had constructed several more reservoirs in Westchester County, in addition to a new aqueduct. The increased supply let the five boroughs expand, and the installation of sewers, flush toilets, and household faucets inevitably led to increased water use. To meet demand, the city in 1905 turned to the Catskills, capturing in reservoirs first the Esopus Creek, then the Rondout and the Schoharie. After drowning nine villages, which bitterly fought the eminent domain proceedings, relocating 2,350 people, and reinterring 3,937 graves, the Catskills system was, in 1928, complete, but not before the city was again on the prowl for more water. This time, engineers impounded branches of the Delaware and Neversink Rivers, at the western edge of the Catskills. The enormous project inundated thirteen communities and displaced another 3,457 people. But the city had doubled its water supply.

It's tempting to compare Fryeburg, which also gives up water for people it never sees, to upstate communities, where resentment against the city still simmers. But while those towns deal with the environmental and social destruction of large dams, they do get something in return: New York City's Department of Environmental Protection pays more than one hundred million dollars a year in property taxes to watershed towns. It also paves roads, develops pollution-prevention plans, builds wastewater treatment plants, and employs more than eighteen hundred people. Fryeburg, so far, enjoys few such benefits from its water exporters.

Today, New York City's tap water originates in watersheds that sprawl over nearly two thousand square miles, filling nineteen reservoirs and three controlled lakes. Twenty-four hours a day, engineers bathed in the glow of cathode-ray tubes flip through computerized maps, charts, and graphs that track every drop of water, its quality and quantity, moving into and out of the system. Not only do they deliver water to the city, they also make allotments for fish conservation (or the trout-fishing industry, however you want to look at it), for "flood mitigation" (lowering reservoirs to make room for storm water), hydroelectric power, independent kayakers, and companies that drop beer-drinking tubers into Esopus Creek in Phoenicia, New York, then pick them up, considerably more relaxed, two hours downstream.

The aesthetic and mechanical beauty of the drinking-water system—95 percent of which is gravity-fed—causes city officials to wax sentimental. "It's miraculous that the system replenishes itself," Commissioner Lloyd tells me as the wind sculpts the surface of the Ashokan and plays with her dark coat. "And if we take care of it, it will provide drinking water for New York forever."

But will we want to drink it?

On a quiet street in Queens on a January morning, Virgilio Tiglao—Tiggy to his friends—lowers the tailgate on his white DEP truck, then opens a silver box that sprouts from the sidewalk at chest height. Inside is a simple spigot, to which he attaches a rubber hose. Tiggy is one of fifteen sample collectors who make the rounds, seven days a week, of 965 monitoring stations within the city. He fills a few containers with Catskill and Delaware water and, on his tailgate, inserts various tools to measure specific conductance (a measure of dissolved mineral content), orthophosphate (which besides inhibiting corrosion is also used, at different concentrations, as a food acidifier and an ingredient in fertilizer), temperature (warmth can indicate stagnant water), and chlorine. His bosses want to see a level of between 0.2 and 4 milligrams per liter.

No one likes the way chlorine tastes or smells (it's detectable to the human nose at 1 milligram per liter), to say nothing of the hazards of transporting or working around deadly chlorine gas, but it seems to be a necessary evil in all surface-water drinking systems. (It's easy to lose the smell: just let your water sit in a jug overnight or pour it back and forth between two containers ten times.) Before chlorine was understood to kill bacteria, people regularly got sick from drinking river and lake water. If they could afford it, they drank bottled groundwater; if they couldn't, they boiled bad water or drank cheap spirits. The widespread use of chlorine in 1920—one of the most important advances in public health—dealt a near-lethal blow to sales of spring and mineral water in this country, but it set the stage for their comeback, based largely on snob appeal, sixty years later.

Finished with his measurements, Tiggy draws additional water samples and drives back to DEP headquarters, a looming office tower in Rego Park that's clad in scaffolding and surrounded by a buzz of civil servants. On the sixth floor, he hands the day's catch to a team of thirty chemists and microbiologists. It's the micro lab's job to find bacteria in the water. And it does—many different types, including the occasional E. coli, which is commonly found in the intestines of animals and humans. Most strains are harmless, but E. coli's presence may indicate inadequate water treatment. If the chlorine is working, however—if it hasn't been blocked by sediment in the water—those bacteria are dead or otherwise deactivated. Federal law allows the presence of live bacteria in up to 5 percent of samples; the city is consistently between 0.1 and 0.2 percent. In 2004, it was revealed that New York's water also contained microscopic crustaceans called copepods, which are found in freshwater and pose no threat to human health. After excruciating debate, Talmudic scholars decided that observant Jews—forbidden by the Torah to consume creeping creatures without fins or scales—need not filter out copepods. But if they chose to filter anyway, doing so on the Sabbath would not violate the prohibition against work.

The copepod caper gave me—and no doubt others—pause. But not for long. In the back of our minds, most New Yorkers understand that we drink water in which fish have their version of sex and pinecones rot. The million-acre watershed doesn't exist in an aseptic vacuum: people park oil-leaking cars around reservoirs, toilets flush into septic tanks that leach into groundwater, and ducks form floating rafts wherever they please. We deal with it. The city's water is nearly pristine, Eric Goldstein, a drinking-water specialist with the Natural Resources Defense Council (NRDC), says. In the world of drinking-water quality, *pristine* means there is no nuclear waste, no MBTE (a gasoline additive), rocket fuel, or landfill leachate in our water. The earth itself filters or neutralizes contaminants, and time is on our side: remember, it takes twelve long months for water to wend from the mountains to our taps.

While the microbiologists do their thing, the chemists check Tiggy's samples for such substances as calcium, magnesium, sodium, nitrate, chloride, silver, iron, and zinc. All water contains some naturally occurring contaminants, such as arsenic or radon. At low levels, says the EPA, they're not "generally" harmful. Some metals and minerals improve the taste—or mouthfeel, as Michael Mascha would put it—of water, and some have nutritional value. At any rate, removing everything that isn't hydrogen and oxygen would put state and local governments, or privately owned utilities, out of business.

When the chemists and microbiologists find contaminant

levels above regulatory standards, they start investigations and sometimes issue boil-water alerts. Until upgrades were made in New York's system, mercury from pressure gauges and seals got into the watershed; so did PCB-laden oil, from gears that open gates and sluiceways. In the late eighties, a high E. coli count led to the discovery that a shed on a reservoir's edge had collapsed in a heavy rainstorm, dumping years' worth of encrusted bird poop into the water. The shed was fixed, extra chlorine went in, and miles of monofilament were strung over the reservoir to keep the creatures from landing.

Tooling around the city's watershed, in the company of civil servants responsible for its health, I see why our water tastes good. The DEP frightens migratory waterfowl off reservoirs, it fixes up homeowners' septic tanks, it collaborates with dairy farmers to control manure runoff and protect stream banks. Most important, it is constantly trying to buy more land, to keep it from the hands of those who would pave and pollute.

But what about the water in cities that control none of their watershed, cities that drink from an enormous river system that serves hundreds of industrial and agricultural communities upstream? What is it like to drink that end product? I decide to visit Kansas City, where the public utility sucks from the Missouri River something that resembles chocolate Yoo-Hoo and turns it into water so good that national magazines shower it with awards and even the locals buy it in bottles.

All natural water has *terroir*, but the water of the Midwest may have a bit more than one might prefer. Pumped from the Missouri, the Mississippi, or any of the Mississippi's many, many tributaries, the water of the heartland is redolent of industrial agriculture, feedlots, ethanol plants, and random industrial enterprises that happen to feed the world. There's grandeur, of a sort, in every gallon. I raise a glass of the Missouri in Kansas City—crystal clear and odor-free—and imagine a beaming row of hardworking civil engineers, chemists, and microbiologists raising their own in salute.

The Kansas City Water Works lies hard by its muddy and meandering source, on the north side of town. Seen from the air, the seventy-acre campus is mostly water: in circular tanks, concrete sluiceways and flumes, and sufficient rectangular pools to cover the flight deck of an aircraft carrier. Through massive pipes, the plant gulps the Missouri, which looks opaque and smells of muck and fish, and holds it for four hours in basins two stories deep. Operators add ferric sulfate and a cationic polymer, which have a positive charge, to neutralize the sediments' electrical charge. The particles clump together and sink. The water's cloudiness—or turbidity—starts to drop from as high as 10,000 NTUs (nephelometric turbidity units) to 50. "If we didn't constantly rake out the sediment, the tank would fill up in a day," Mike Klender, a stocky civil engineer who manages the plant, tells me as we gaze into an empty basin receiving its biannual power wash.

The water leaves the primary tanks in a flume, where potassium permanganate is added to counteract bad tastes and smells from, well, everything upstream. Then a disinfecting cocktail of chlorine and ammonia—called chloramine—is added, then lime, to soften the water and raise its pH, which helps particles coagulate and settle out. Now whitish gray, the water spends some time in softening basins, where organics and chemicals combine to form a froth of *floaties*, which look like clumps of sheep's wool. The floaties contain viruses and bacteria. "They get bigger and bigger until they sink," Klender says. Reconsidering his description, he adds, "What we're trying to create is an aggressive aggregate moment."

After the moment passes, the water flows placidly through wooden walls into a field of secondary tanks, where it's suddenly, startlingly, blue. The NTU isn't yet 0.1—well below the federal standard—but it's getting there. On this ninety-degree day, I find the urge to dive into these thirty million gallons of sparkling turquoise water nearly irresistible. The water looks done to me, but Klender has further plans. After spending four hours in the secondary tanks, the water will be dosed with carbon dioxide in an adjacent basin, to lower its pH (water with a high pH tastes dry, Klender says), and, depending on the season, blended with powder-activated carbon, which turns all that blue temporarily black.

"The carbon absorbs atrazine," Klender says.

Every year, American farmers spread about seventy-six million pounds of atrazine, a herbicide, on fields. When it rains, much of that runs into ditches and streams, contaminating drinking-water sources in nearly every major Midwestern city, and well water and groundwater in states where the compound isn't even used. Scientists with the U.S. Geological Survey (USGS) have found atrazine at levels up to 224 parts per billion in some Midwestern streams. When Breck Speed, CEO of Mountain Valley Spring Company, looked around Missouri for a spring to feed a bottling plant—water companies are always looking to expand, I'm learning—he came up dry: all the groundwater he tested contained atrazine.

Atrazine kills weeds, and more. Even at levels well below the federal standard—three parts per billion—it causes birth defects, reproductive disorders, and cancer in lab animals. (In the European Union, the maximum contaminant level for atrazine is thirty times lower, at 0.1 ppb.) Human kidneys filter atrazine, and most people don't spend a lot of time swimming in herbicide-laced water, as frogs do. But human fetuses *do* live in water. When I asked Tyrone Hayes, the Berkeley developmental endocrinologist who discovered that atrazine caused male frogs, in the wild and in the lab, to grow ovaries in their testes, if he'd recommend that his pregnant wife or his children drink tap water in the Midwest in the springtime, he said, "Why take that chance?"

How do cities get away with serving atrazine-laced water? It's simple: water utilities are required to announce to the feds only their quarterly averages. EPA regulations focus on limiting risks from long-term exposure: levels of atrazine may peak in the May-to-August runoff period, but with averaging out over quarters, it's possible to come in under the wire. Cities can also test before and after predicted spikes. The New Orleans Sewerage and Water Board, which takes raw water from the Mississippi River, tells customers its "running annual averages observed have always been found to be below the Maximum Contaminant Levels (MCLs) set by the EPA." Kansas City, by contrast, has never topped three parts per billion in a *day*, let alone averaged over a year.

And then there's this: the government sets standards for most contaminants based on a healthy 150-pound person who drinks two liters of water a day. "If you drink a lot more, you get a higher exposure," Jane Houlihan of the Environmental Working Group, says. "Or if you're small or vulnerable to a contaminant, you're also at higher risk."

Houlihan reminds me that when the EPA sets standards for drinking water, it balances health effects—how many people would get sick from a contaminant—with the cost of cleaning up water to reduce that risk. Pesticide regulations for fruits and vegetables, by contrast, are only health-based. Federal law requires the EPA to prove that the cost of removing a contaminant doesn't exceed its benefits (deaths averted, that is, with a human life valued at $6.1 million). If it does, the legal limits are raised—that is, weakened.

Agricultural impacts on drinking water are bound to get worse. Pushed by the ethanol boom that drove up corn prices, farmers in 2007 planted ninety million acres of corn, 15 percent more than the previous year. All that corn will probably be treated with atrazine; the new hybrid and genetically modified varieties also require more fertilizer than any other major crop. Inevitably, heavy rains wash excess nitrogen and phosphorus, from commercial fertilizer and from animal waste applied as fertilizer, into groundwater and surface water. And so a fuel that is supposed to help us drive cleaner—by reducing our reliance on oil—is likely to make our water dirtier.

In reservoirs and rivers across the country, these excess nutrients encourage the growth of algae. When algae die, bacteria feed on the dead plants and consume the oxygen in the water. These anaerobic conditions strangle aquatic life in reservoirs and have created a nearly 8,000-square-mile "dead zone" in the Gulf of Mexico, into which the Mississippi River drains. Low-oxygen conditions also release iron and manganese previously bound to bottom sediments. Water taste, odor, and color quickly go downhill (the technical term is *skunked*). It gets worse: dead algae and bacteria, along with other organic material, combine with chlorine in treated water to form a polysyllabic array of potential carcinogens in drinking water. These disinfection by-products—trihalomethanes and haloacetic acids—have been linked to an increased risk of bladder cancer and miscarriage. In cities such as New York, levels of disinfection by-products typically increase by as much as 1.5 to 2 times during summer months, when there's more organic material in the water and plant operators dispense more chlorine.

Klender doesn't worry about nitrogen—there's so much water in the Missouri that by the time he takes his cut, levels are fairly dilute. "Got it covered" is his general attitude: with enough chemicals and technology, it seems, he can handle anything. Other cities aren't so lucky. Des Moines, which drinks from the Raccoon and Des Moines Rivers, was forced to build a $4.5 million de-nitrification plant (which costs three grand a day to run) to comply with federal requirements. Iowa communities that drink from shallow wells, and that lack funds for fancy ion-exchange systems, have a tougher time of it. When nitrates spike, they issue "blue baby" alerts. (Nitrates in water bind to hemoglobin in babies' blood, hindering its ability to deliver oxygen to the brain. In adults, high nitrate levels have been linked with increased risk of hyperthyroidism, birth defects, and spontaneous abortions.)

Ethanol plants themselves, the destination for about a fifth of the corn crop in 2007, will affect both water quantity and quality. Producing one gallon of the alternative fuel requires about four gallons of water: a facility making 100 million gallons a year, then, would need about 400 million gallons of water. Iowa water managers worry that most of the state's twenty-seven ethanol plants will be pulling that water from deep aquifers that provide drinking water to the state. So worried are water managers in Nebraska, the nation's number three corn producer, that some workers spend their days whacking phragmites and other water-sucking plants from wetlands to save water for other uses.

The ethanol industry says that more than half the water it uses either evaporates or is treated and released to streams. But the plants' wastewater, Susan Heathcote, water program director of the Iowa Environmental Council, says, "can be more like brine. They use reverse osmosis to purify their water"—forcing water at high pressure through a semipermeable membrane—"and they end up with high concentrations of sulfides, chloride, and iron." Diluted sufficiently in big streams, the contaminants are harmless, but many plants discharge into creeks that contain little water.

Ethanol worries Klender only if it means more atrazine will be washing from cornfields. It's his job to lower levels, sometimes as high as 35 ppb, to less than 3. It costs him thirty-six thousand dollars to fill an empty silo with carbon (which also removes oil and pesticides from water), and he goes through as many as five silo loads a year. "Yep," he says, "atrazine is a real pain for us."

I look at the basin where the carbon goes in. "What do you do with the atrazine once you filter it out?"

"We put it back in the river." It will be the city of Boonville's problem next.

A public road and a thin band of woods parallel the settling tanks. "We once had a deer in the tank," Klender says. "It jumped over the fence and Rusty"—a large man with ranch experience, currently poking at a weir with a long tool—"lassoed him out." Did you have to clean out the tanks?

"Nope." Again, volume.

Colleen Newman, a public information officer who's tagging along with Klender and me, remembers another intrusion. "A car went by and someone lobbed a small object into the secondary tanks. We had to shut them down for two days while we ran all the tests."

"What was it?"

"A Baby Ruth bar."

She says it so straight-faced, I don't have the nerve to ask if she's referencing the scene in *Caddyshack* where a Baby Ruth in a pool is mistaken for fecal matter.

Fouling a system this large isn't something the waterworks frets about. "You'd need barges and barges of contaminants to affect the system," Klender says. When I'd arrived this morning, a security guard stopped me; after I told him my name, he moved two plastic cones so I could drive in.

From the final basin, post-atrazine-treatment, operators add fluoride, then another polymer to bind bits of calcium carbonate to each other so they can be filtered. Next comes sodium hexametaphosphate, to halt that reaction: Klender wants to keep some lime in solution so it can coat distribution pipes, a prophylactic against the leaching of lead and other metals. And then it's on to the grandly named filter gallery, where Kansas City's drinking water drops slowly through forty-two inches of gravel, torpedo sand, and filter sand before coming to rest in multimillion-gallon underground reservoirs. The water is about to disappear from my view, so I take a good look at the filter area. As microbes and other debris collect atop the sand, which I can't actually see, they form a thick layer that was called, years ago, a *Schmutzdecke*—German for "filth cover." It sounds gross, but it's essential for the filter to work properly. Like nothing else in the plant, I realize, the filtering process mimics, in a supercondensed time frame, the purifying processes of nature. It's the same ecosystem service provided for free in such places as Fryeburg, Maine, by glacier-made beds of sand and gravel.

After four to eight hours in the underground reservoir, during which time the chloramines blossom to their fullest disinfecting power, Klender's water is pumped north and south to Missourians up to forty miles away.

Before saying good-bye to my guides, I take a quick sip from an indoor fountain, serving possibly the freshest water (short of rain) in Kansas City. I think about all the trouble the utility takes to clean the Missouri River, and I wonder how many of its labors could have been avoided—with better land-use planning, better agricultural practices, and a lot more monitoring and enforcement upstream. After all, if the bad stuff didn't go in, we wouldn't have to take it out.

As I refill my water bottle for the road, I realize that what had once seemed so simple and natural, a drink of water, is neither. All my preconceptions about this most basic of beverages have been queered. Soon, they'll be turned upside down.

Chapter 6

AFTERTASTE

A<small>LMOST ALL U.S.</small> communities with a public drinking-water supply are required by the EPA to publish annual consumer confidence, or "right to know," reports. They contain a lot of technical language about microbial parameters and maximum contaminant levels and goals, and without an understanding of government rule-making—and excellent eyesight—it's natural to assume that everything is fine. After all, 89.3 percent of the country's nearly fifty-three thousand public water systems met or exceeded federal standards for health and safety in 2006. We haven't had a major outbreak of waterborne illness in fifteen years, and you can travel pretty much anywhere in this country, open the tap, and drink without fear that you'll soon be bolting for the bathroom.

For that we can thank the managers of water plants, who aren't a celebrated lot. They play the hand they are dealt, in terms of source water, and if they do their job well, few notice. If they're in the news, it's because something went massively wrong. Mike Klender makes it sound easy to make good water from oil spills, industrial discharges, agricultural runoff, animal waste, treated sewage, and raw sewage (more than 850 billion gallons of which flow into U.S. waterways each year from overburdened systems). But it's not simple, and many utilities struggle.

In 1993, both Washington, D.C., and New York City found unacceptable levels of E. coli in their water supplies. To protect the public from such outbreaks, the EPA in 2002 began requiring cities that drink unfiltered surface water to use two disinfection methods instead of one. Some cities opted to kill pathogens by exposing their water to ozone, an extreme oxidant. Others decided to run their water past lamps emitting ultraviolet radiation. Both methods are far cheaper than filtering. When New York completes its UV plant, in 2010, it will be the largest in the world.

"It's a belt-and-suspenders approach," Alan Steinberg, the EPA administrator whose region of responsibility includes New York and New Jersey, says. Ultraviolet light, Steven Schindler, New York City's director of drinking-water quality control, tells me when I visit DEP headquarters in Queens, "inactivates" cryptosporidium, a microscopic parasite that can cause disease but is resistant to chlorine.

"You mean it kills the crypto?"

Schindler hesitates. "It destroys their ability to reproduce." Either dead or sterile, they can do us no harm.

Cryptosporidium occurs in 65 to 97 percent of surface waters in the United States, according to the Centers for Disease Control and Prevention. In 1993, more than four hundred thousand people were sickened, and sixty-nine people died, when the parasite made its way from farms and forests into Lake Michigan and then into Milwaukee's drinking-water supply. The city has since tightened its purification and testing procedures and added ozone disinfection. Investigations showed that New York's crypto comes not from human poop but from deer, opossum, and skunk—which I find strangely reassuring.

Using ultraviolet light lets utilities cut back their use of chlorine, which, again, reacts with organic material to form disinfection by-products. All cities wrestle with the right formula: use too little chlorine and microbes survive. Use too much, and you get potential carcinogens. "Disinfectants limit microbial risk; infectious disease is the major concern," says Robert D. Morris, an environmental epidemiologist and the author of *The Blue Death: Disease, Disaster, and the Water We Drink*, which both defends and attacks our drinking-water system. "If people get cancer in twenty to thirty years, no one is going to take the water department to task for that. So water managers aren't anxious to see new rules that lower disinfection by-products." (A Brita filter, like other pitchers certified by the NSF/ANSI Standard 42, will substantially reduce some of these chlorine by-products, but it won't eliminate any of them. Brita is, by the way, owned by the Clorox Company.)

Nearly a third of water utilities in the nation, Kansas City included, have thrown in the towel, switching from chlorine to the chlorine-and-ammonia mixture known as chloramine. But this compound has downsides too. For one thing, chloramine isn't as strong a disinfectant as chlorine. To remove sludge and sediment from its pipes, Washington, D.C., which switched to chloramines in 2004, annually conducts a good old-fashioned "chlorine burn." The high dose, predictably, increases levels of disinfection by-products. Utility officials maintain that D.C. water, which comes from the Potomac, still meets EPA safety standards because levels are averaged over the year.

Second, some studies suggest chloramines create their own toxic by-products, few of which have been thoroughly studied. One of these, reported a team of researchers in 2004, is more toxic to mammalian cells than any other disinfection by-product. Some residents of the Bay Area have complained of burning rashes and asthma attacks after showering in water treated with the stuff. No studies have directly linked cause and effect; investigations are ongoing. Third, chloramines can make water caustic, which in turn leaches lead from older pipes and fittings. Ingesting lead can cause serious health and developmental problems, including learning disabilities and behavioral problems in children, as well as kidney problems and high blood pressure in adults. One recent study showed an association between toddlers with high lead levels and violent crime when those toddlers grow up.

In Washington, D.C., the switch to chloramines exposed tens of thousands of residents to lead at three hundred parts per billion. The EPA "action level," above which utilities must take mitigating steps, is 15 ppb. As of mid-2007, the city had replaced about a third of its lead service lines, which connect mains to individual water meters. Whenever I speak to water experts in the capital region, whether in government, in academia, or at advocacy groups, I ask what they drink. Always it's tap; always, they run it through either a pour-through or on-tap filter.

Seattle, San Francisco, and Portland, Oregon, own their entire watersheds, which means they're generally protected from developers and industry. But coliform bacteria—from animals and from humans—still make their way into the water. That's life. New York City controls less than 50 percent of its watershed (Boston slightly more than 50 percent), and roughly one hundred wastewater treatment plants dump their effluent into streams that lead to reservoirs. The practice is more common than one might think: more than two hundred municipalities, including Las Vegas, discharge billions of gallons of sewage into the Colorado River, which supplies drinking water to San Diego and other cities. All down the Missouri and the Mississippi, towns drink from, and discharge back into, the river. New Orleans, at the bottom of the Mighty Miss, drinks the effluent of nearly half the U.S. urban population. But those discharges are first filtered and disinfected at wastewater treatment plants, then diluted in the river before they're sucked up by drinking-water plants, which treat the water again before sending it out to taps.

New York City is trying to upgrade all the sewage plants in its watershed to state-of-the-art "tertiary" treatment, but more than two dozen of them still use suboptimal "secondary" cleaning. Of the effluent from the more advanced plants, Steven Schindler says, "I've heard of plant operators drinking it on a tour."

This information lifts the eyebrows of the NRDC's Eric Goldstein. "It's very clean for *sewage* water," Goldstein says, practically hidden behind towers of reports, legal pads, newspaper clippings, and memos on his desk in Manhattan, "but you'd have to be a nut to do that." Goldstein reminds me—and I really do want to believe him—that the city's water settles for months, and it's enormously diluted. He hops up to grab a thick book. "Here we go," he says, flipping through the pages. "Ten point five million gallons of sewage a day goes into the system." That sounds like a lot (it would fill nearly sixteen Olympic-size swimming pools), but the reservoirs hold about 550 billion gallons of water, of which the city takes 1.2 billion gallons (1,817 swimming pools) a day. The ratio of sewage to nonsewage, in other words, is sub-homeopathic.

The thing is, chlorine is supposed to take care of that effluent, the bad stuff that makes it out the discharge pipe. But creeping levels of sediment in the reservoirs can block disinfection. Sediment can also serve as food for disease-causing organisms. In general, the higher the turbidity, the higher the risk that water drinkers will develop gastrointestinal diseases. In New York, the problem started decades ago, when developers began clearing more land in the Catskills, paving more surfaces, and building more roads, all of which increase erosion and speed the flow of sediment into creeks and streams that run into the reservoirs. Climate change, in the form of stronger and more frequent storms, has made turbidity much worse.

The EPA says turbidity may never exceed one nephelometric turbidity unit in 95 percent of daily samples in any month, but some researchers think the bar is set too high—that people get sick at even lower values. A study conducted in the early nineties in Philadelphia found that emergency room visits and hospital admissions for children with gastrointestinal illnesses increased by about 10 percent whenever the turbidity of the city's filtered water supply increased significantly (but was still in compliance with current federal standards). And about ten days after the spikes in turbidity, hospital admissions of the elderly for GI illnesses increased by 9 percent.

To counteract the increased levels of particulate matter, cities have long dumped aluminum sulfate, or alum, into the water. It makes the particles clump together and sink. But alum is no panacea. Heavy use can make water more acidic, and acidic water can corrode pipes. Over the years, so much alum has accumulated on the bottom of New York's Kensico Reservoir, in Westchester County, that it's now smothering aquatic life. For many nail-biting months, the city wondered if the EPA would grant the city its next filtration avoidance permit (the previous five-year permit had expired). If the DEP couldn't get a handle on sediment—perhaps by retrofitting its dams and weirs to give water more time to settle—it would have to build a filtration plant so vast it would cover an area larger than fifteen football fields.

Filtering Catskill-Delaware water would be a blow to New Yorkers' water pride (the city is currently building a filter plant for its Croton system, which collects water from densely developed watersheds east of the Hudson), but the financial impact, according to James Tierney, the state assistant attorney general charged with enforcing environmental laws within the watershed, would be "like a bomb going off." The plant would cost more than six billion dollars to build, and the cost of staffing, operation, maintenance, and debt service would reach one billion dollars annually. After examining the city's watershed protection plan and accepting public comment, the EPA decided to grant the permit. The city's comptroller, no doubt, said, "Phew."

After publishing an article on New York's water system, which mentioned chlorine's deadly effect on E. coli, I receive a long telephone message from a gentleman in California. The gist of Frank Pecarich's pitch is that chlorine doesn't kill all bacteria. He refers me to studies conducted by the U.S. Department of Agriculture's Agricultural Research Service, which found that a particularly virulent strain of E. coli, called 0157:H7, can survive the most stringent wastewater treatment process and then evade standard tests.

"The E. coli has learned to go into an inactive state," Pecarich says when I call him. Pecarich is a former USDA soil scientist, and he's apparently devoted his retirement to fighting the use of treated wastewater in agriculture, a common practice in California's Monterey County. "They form biofilms in pipes. They feed on bacteria in the water, and then they reemerge even stronger." Bill Costerton, a microbiologist at the University of Southern California who coined the word *biofilms*, describes them as highly structured communities of bacterial cells living cooperatively and excreting gluey slime that helps them adhere to surfaces—on medical implants, on soil particles, and in water pipes.

It takes as few as ten organisms of 0157:H7, which grow in the rumens of cattle, for an infection, Pecarich says. The strain secretes a powerful poison, called a verotoxin, that can lead to bloody diarrhea, kidney failure, and death. Tertiary sewage treatment gets water 99.7 percent clean, Pecarich says, "but the number of pathogens is so huge that 0.3 percent can kill you." That is, if you're vulnerable: young, old, or with a compromised immune system. In May of 2000, approximately two thousand people in Walkerton, Ontario, were infected with 0157:H7 in the municipal water supply, of whom seven died. In 2006, 0157:H7 killed at least three people and sickened more than two hundred in the United States after they ate spinach irrigated with treated wastewater. That same year, more than 150 people who dined at Taco Bell were sickened by the bacterium.

When I get off the phone with Pecarich, I draw a mental map that leads from cow to consumer, from toilet to tap. Grain-fed cows grow 0157:H7 in their gut (most bacteria are killed by the acid of a cow's stomach juice, but the 0157:H7 strain is resistant to strong acids; its incidence falls dramatically when cows are placed on their natural diet of hay and forage). The pathogen works its way from slaughterhouses into hamburgers (in 1993, more than seven hundred people became ill, and four children died, from eating contaminated meat at Jack in the Box restaurants; in 2007, the Topps Meat Company recalled 21.7 million pounds of ground beef after its hamburger, tainted with 0157:H7, sickened forty people in eight states). Sick people use their toilets, and the bacteria enter wastewater treatment plants. From there, the treated water goes into irrigation pipes and out onto the leafy greens. Or up the intake pipes of city drinking-water systems.

So there is shit in the water; I'd have to make peace with that (though not, perhaps, with grain-fed cows). I'm not in a high-risk group, the bacteria are few and far between, and they are dead (except, perhaps, for the 0157: H7). But what about the other contaminants that regularly show up in tap water, things like heavy metals?

Arsenic is a known human carcinogen. The EPA's drinking-water goal for the metal is zero, but goals, in the bureaucracy of drinking water, are aspirational. They can't be enforced. Today, the maximum contaminant level for arsenic is ten parts per billion, and more than fifty-six million Americans drink water that exceeds this level. Arsenic gets into water from naturally occurring deposits in rocks and soil (remember, water is a universal solvent: it picks up traces of substances—such as metals or minerals—wherever it roams). It's also released to the environment through industry and agriculture (arsenic is a component of poultry feed). The element is used as a wood preservative, and in paints, dyes, metals, drugs, soaps, and semiconductors—all things routinely buried in landfills, which generate arsenic-tainted leachate. Arsenic is also an ingredient in some fertilizers, fungicides, insecticides, and rodenticides, which readily contaminate groundwater.

Arsenic in water doesn't smell or taste like anything, so you'll know it's in there only if you test for it. Or await the consequences: high levels have been associated with thickening and discoloration of the skin, stomach pain, nausea, vomiting, and diarrhea in the short term; and numbness in hands and feet, partial paralysis, and blindness over the longer term. Arsenic has been linked to cancer of the bladder, lungs, skin, kidney, nasal passages, liver, and prostate. And it has an exalted place in the literature of intentional poisoning: it takes less than two ounces to kill a 150-pound person. A twelve-foot-long two-by-six that's pressure treated with arsenic contains enough poison to kill two hundred adults if you burn the board and feed its ash to the crowd.

How do you tell if you've been exposed to a dangerous dose of arsenic? It's relatively simple: you clip a sample of your hair or finger- or toenail, and send it to a lab. But then what? The test can't tell you whether you'll get cancer, and there's no treatment for exposure, only relief from symptoms of illness.

In January of 2006, the EPA lowered its arsenic standard from fifty parts per billion to ten (about the equivalent of ten drops of ink in an Olympic-size swimming pool, or ten kernels of corn in a forty-foot silo). Municipal systems and residential wells over the limit were shut down. Towns that can't hold polluters accountable are forced to switch sources, truck in water from other locations, or provide bottled water to residents. People who drink from private wells, of course, are on their own, in terms of both testing their water (which can cost upwards of one hundred dollars, depending on how many tests you order) and dealing with the results.

It is possible to get arsenic out of water. Pour-through filters (such as a Brita or a PUR) don't do the job, but reverse-osmosis filters certified by NSF (a nonprofit group that develops public-health and safety standards and tests) claim to remove the metal but don't guarantee it. Another option is on the horizon, but it probably won't scale up for city systems: *Pteris vittata*, or ladder brake fern, has been found to soak up arsenic through its roots, which grow in either soil or water, and store the metal in its fronds. But what to do with the toxic fronds?

Either seal them in airtight containers, says Edenspace, a Virginia-based company that licenses the patent for the ferns and sells them commercially, or dispose of them in a hazardous-waste facility. One can only hope that this facility never leaches into groundwater, and thence into wells.

Not everyone is happy with the feds' arsenic limits, but at least arsenic *has* a standard. So political is the debate over the health effects of perchlorate, an ingredient of rocket fuel, that the EPA hasn't set allowable levels for the chemical in drinking water. But it's there.

Perchlorate contaminates the water sources of between eleven and twenty million people across the country, mainly in areas where the Department of Defense manufactured weapons and rocket fuel. Before production stopped in 1998, the Kerr-McGee plant in Henderson, Nevada, manufactured thirty thousand tons of the chemical each month. After perchlorate was discovered in the Colorado River, the company initiated a one-hundred-million-dollar cleanup program. As of April 2005, pumps and filters had removed more than three million pounds of perchlorate from groundwater, but the chemical still enters the river daily, tainting the drinking water of people in Nevada, Arizona, and California. "It is really one of the most massive pollution problems the water industry has ever seen," Timothy Brick, of the Metropolitan Water District of Southern California, told *High Country News* during the cleanup.

By interfering with the ability of the thyroid gland to produce hormones that control growth and metabolism, perchlorate disrupts normal brain development in fetuses and infants. (Not surprisingly, it's also used to treat hyperthyroidism.) Some studies say the chemical can cause thyroid tumors in adults, but it's pregnant women and infants—the usual suspects—who are most strongly warned to steer clear of perchlorate-laced water. Advocacy groups as well as scientific experts at the EPA, and Congresswoman Hilda L. Solis from California, have pressured the Bush administration to set a federal drinking-water standard for perchlorate that is protective of prebirth and newborn infants. So far, no luck. The process seems hopelessly mired in politics. On one hand you've got sufficient evidence that rocket fuel in drinking water is a health hazard; and on the other hand, you've got enormously powerful aerospace and defense industries not thrilled to spend billions on cleanups. (As with arsenic, reverse osmosis removes perchlorate from tap water, but carbon filtering doesn't.)

Farther east, underground plumes of perfluorochemicals (PFC), a compound linked with organ damage, contaminate private and municipal wells in twenty-five communities around Minneapolis. Unregulated by the federal government, PFCs have also been found in New Jersey, West Virginia, and North Carolina.

In twenty-four states, the U.S. Geological Survey has found methyl tertiary butyl ether, aka MTBE, in groundwater. A gasoline additive that reduces carbon monoxide and ozone levels caused by auto emissions, it works its way into the environment from leaking underground storage tanks (known in the biz as LUST), and from pipeline spills and emissions from motorboats on lakes and reservoirs. At high doses, MTBE gives rats cancer. Should we worry about drinking it? Unclear. The EPA has convened a blue-ribbon panel to research the costs and benefits of regulation. For now, the chemical lingers on the agency's Contaminant Candidate List. The bill for cleaning soil and water of MTBE could reach thirty billion dollars, nationally.

In December of 2005, the Environmental Working Group (EWG) released a report, following a two-and-a-half-year investigation, that found tap water in forty-two states was contaminated with 141 chemicals for which the government had failed to set safety standards. That's 141 contaminants in addition to the 114 already under scrutiny. (Others suggest the sky's the limit when it comes to unregulated contaminants—industry pumps out new ones faster than regulating agencies can test them.) The unregulated contaminants are linked to cancer, reproductive toxicity, developmental toxicity, and immune system damage. They come from industry (plasticizers, solvents, and propellants), from agriculture (fertilizer and pesticide ingredients), from development (runoff polluted by auto emissions and lawn chemicals, and effluent from sewage treatment plants), and from water treatment itself. Yes, cleaning up the water to decrease microbial illness—with chlorine, chloramines, ozone, and other chemicals—can cause problems of its own, in some cases increasing the risk of cancer and developmental and reproductive disorders. It's enough to make a tap lover cry.

Still, Arthur Ashendorf, a former head of New York City's drinking-water-quality program, dismisses the EWG report as "crazy." He adds, "There's always someone looking for something wrong." Cynthia Dougherty, director of the EPA's Office of Ground Water and Drinking Water, agrees that source water needs more protection, but found the report "overstates the need for concern" and "raises unnecessary alarm." The libertarian Competitive Enterprise Institute calls the report nothing but "hype" because the contaminants "appear infrequently at such low levels that it makes them inconsequential."

Unfortunately, that isn't always true. Scientists are learning that smaller and smaller amounts of chemicals are anything but inconsequential; that exposure to minute traces of the wrong chemical at the wrong time—at critical stages of fetal or child development, for example—can cause more harm than large doses later in life. Moreover, none of these contaminants come to us solo, like a single coffee ground floating in a glass of water. In forty-two states, people drink tap water that contains at least ten different pollutants on the same day. Looking at end points that include immune and reproductive system dysfunctions and neurological, cognitive, and behavioral effects—instead of just cancer—researchers are finding that mixtures of chemicals can induce these effects in much smaller concentrations than do single chemicals, and that low-level exposure can often induce results not seen at higher levels.

If scientists know there's potential trouble in our drinking water, why isn't the government doing anything? In fact, the EPA has a list of fifty-one microbial and chemical contaminants that it's considering regulating. But it's expensive to identify and detect these contaminants, to determine their health effects, and then to treat the water. Any changes are likely to require massive capital projects with long lead times—exactly the sort of projects that drinking-water plant managers, concerned with meeting current state standards, are unlikely to propose to their boss, who's usually an elected official. Moreover, any ultimate improvements in drinking water are unlikely to be noticed by the folks who will end up paying for it. All in all, not a formula for improvement.

At the tail end of the nineties, the USGS began using highly sensitive assays to test American waterways for something they'd never considered before: drugs. In 2002, the agency announced it had found traces of eighty-two different contaminants, including natural and synthetic hormones, antibiotics, antihypertensives, painkillers, and antidepressants. The researchers also found caffeine, nicotine, and the residue of personal-care products such as shampoo, sunscreen, and insecticide. The stuff was just about everywhere: in rural and urban areas, in wells, surface water, and groundwater. Drugs were leaking from septic tanks (every time we pop a pill, its metabolites show up in our excreta), flowing off animal feedlots, and pouring into rivers from wastewater treatment plants.

The levels of pharmaceuticals found in drinking water are infinitesimally low, in the range of parts per billion or parts per trillion. But their supplies are continually replenished. Scientists have recently made the connection between hormones in water and abnormalities in fish: males are growing female sex tissue. Like most pharmaceuticals, hormones aren't designed to break down easily. They're supposed to have an effect at low dosages with chronic use, and they only partly dissolve in water.

According to a report by the International Union of Pure and Applied Chemistry and the Scientific Committee on Problems of the Environment, a worldwide network of scientists and scientific institutions, more than two hundred species—aquatic and terrestrial—are known or suspected to have experienced adverse reactions to such endocrine disrupters as estrogen and its many synthetic mimics. But what are the effects on people?

In the United Kingdom, hormones in the environment have been linked with lowered sperm counts and gynecomastia—the development of breasts in men. A benign condition, gynecomastia is also on the rise in the United States. And breast cancer in males—linked with estrogen in both males and females—rose 26 percent between 1973 and 1998. The incidence of hypospadias, a birth defect of the penis, has increased in the United States and other countries; scientists have linked the condition to fetal exposure to endocrine-disrupting chemicals. In some Arctic villages, twice as many girls as boys are being born: scientists with the Arctic Monitoring and Assessment Programme link the skewed sex ratio to the mothers' diet of walrus, seals, and polar bears, which consume estrogen-mimicking chemicals in their own diet.

What if the EPA, which is studying chemicals that interfere with the endocrine system, finds that they constitute a serious risk to human health? Wastewater treatment plants aren't designed to remove hormones, to say nothing of traces of antidepressants, painkillers, and the plasticizers found in shampoo and other types of plastic bottles. But that doesn't mean they can't. The technology is out there, says Lynn Orphan, former president of the Water Environment Federation, which represents operators of municipal wastewater-treatment plants. "We can use activated carbon or membrane filters, which have tiny pores. There's reverse-osmosis filtration and exposure to ozone or to ultraviolet light. Sometimes it's just a matter of extra retention time in holding tanks."

But the technologies aren't cheap, especially when scaled up for day-to-day use on an entire city's water. Hugh Kaufman, a senior policy analyst on waste issues at the EPA, says, "The cost of putting them in place, plus their operation, is astronomical—hundreds of millions over the lifetime of a plant." Kansas City's Mike Klender, like other water-plant operators, has little to say about pharmaceuticals. The government doesn't require him to look for or control them, and so he does neither.

Let's say your drinking water is pristine: it contains no disinfection by-products, no traces of fertilizer or pesticides, no industrial pollutants, and respectably low levels of naturally occurring elements such as zinc, arsenic, sodium, and radon. Maybe you live in Fryeburg, Maine, where the water that goes into town pipes is pretty close to the water that goes into Poland Spring's tanker trucks. Or maybe you live in Kansas City. You still might not want to drink that water if the pipes leading to your house look like hell.

While utilities are responsible for the condition of the water they deliver to your home, the service lines that bring water up to your taps, and the water-storage system in your building, are the responsibility of the landlord. It was common, up through the 1940s, to use lead service lines to connect city water mains to residential buildings. And lead solder was used to join pipes until the mideighties, when it was banned (outlaw plumbers, of course, might still have used it). Letting the water run for five minutes at the start of the day flushes lead, but it contradicts a lifetime's public service messages to conserve water, and it seriously interferes with production of the morning's first cup of coffee.

Nearly every week, a town or a school or an office building discovers high lead levels in its drinking water. Residents are advised to switch to alternative sources—including bottled water—until pipes can be replaced. (Boiling water doesn't reduce lead content.) Other minerals and metals—such as calcium, magnesium, copper, and iron—can corrode and clog pipes with structures called tubercles that can snag passing microorganisms. Imagine the lungs of a TB patient, add a lot of orange, green, and red, and you get the picture: yuck. The image was driven home when I spoke to a gentleman hawking an innovative pipe-scrubbing-and-coating system. "I've seen some pipes so filled with gunk," he said, "they're only a quarter-inch wide"—a tenth of their original diameter.

"Do you drink your tap water?" I asked.

"Are you kidding? The last time they cleaned out the water tank on my roof they found dead pigeons in it."

Dead animals aren't good, but most bacteria aren't bad. Of course, their habit of multiplying and making themselves at home in water infrastructure isn't completely appetizing. In a lecture he gave in September of 2000, Bill Costerton, the biofilms researcher, warned, "Never pull the casing on your well and look at it because you have been drinking water that has been coming over a filthy-looking mess with all kinds of oscillating slime fibers and so on. The best bet so far . . . is to keep your biofilm healthy, don't have it coming off, keep it well fed, don't antagonize it, don't hit [it] with any chlorine. But it is a ticklish situation when you think about it. There is something living down there and you have to keep it happy or it will do bad things for you."

Among the things that can live in biofilms "down there," according to Marc Edwards, a MacArthur award–winning civil engineer at Virginia Tech, are *Legionella,* which causes Legionnaires' disease, and nontuberculous mycobacterium, which can cause pulmonary disease resembling tuberculosis, and other diseases. "Hot-water storage tanks and showerheads may permit the amplification of these bacteria," Edwards writes.

To reach the holding tanks of New York City, upstate water runs through two massive tunnels. When chemists for the Department of Environmental Protection found biofilms in those conduits, their supervisors tried to suppress the report. "And so the chemists handed their reports to us," Bill Wegner, watershed analyst for the environmental advocacy group Riverkeeper, tells me. Eventually, Wegner says, the biofilms will need remediation: "They'll slough off, or they'll choke the system." Fortunately, the city is nearing the final stages of building a third water tunnel, an enormous (more than sixty miles long) and expensive (between $5.5 billion and $6 billion) undertaking that began with a dynamite blast in 1970. The opening of the third tunnel in 2012 will allow the inspection and repair of the other tunnels for the first time since they opened, one in 1917 and the other in 1935.

When I come home from long weekends away, I notice a thin brownish fog at the bottom of my Brita UltraMax, which holds a gallon of water and sits atop my fridge. I'd inherited the tank years ago and used it not out of fear (my attitude, until recently at least, was "What, me worry?") but because it removes the water's chlorine edge. My consumer confidence report, put out by the city's Department of Environmental Protection, says this fuzz is iron oxide from the distribution pipes, and that sudden changes in the system—for example, when a fire hydrant is opened—can stir up sediments and cause temporary discoloration. But my sediment is visible whenever the water sits for several days, leaving me to wonder if it is always there, but suspended. (My water, according to the DEP, contains less than the legal limit of iron.) But why isn't the Brita catching it?

"I've never seen that," Sylvie Chavanne, research-and-development group manager for Brita, tells me when I phone. "But we don't claim to remove iron."

And then there is the spigot of the tank. Once or twice I've noticed a tiny vegetal blob just poking from its snout. Is it an oscillating slime fiber? Do I need to buy my own pig? Is my filter's *Schmutzdecke* too schmutzy? When I remember, I clean the plastic spigot with a tiny brush, but the stainless steel pipes of Dasani, Aquafina, and Poland Spring are starting to look better and better. Maybe taking personal responsibility for my water system isn't such a great idea after all.

A lot can go wrong with your home's plumbing, but even more goes wrong in the streets. Every year, according to the American Water Works Association, between 250,000 and 300,000 water mains break. Sometimes freezing and cracking damages pipes, sometimes construction workers are to blame. Ruptured pipes send geysers of filth into the sky, white water runs down the streets, and taps go dry. Any time a pipe breaks, pressure drops, and water managers contemplate the possibility of contaminants leaking into the system. Flooding, too, can swamp and contaminate water systems. Toward the end of 2006, severe storms stirred up so much sediment in Vancouver reservoirs that the city went on boil-water alert for more than a week. Fights broke out in stores over bottled water, Starbucks stopped serving drinks made with water, and hotels added more chlorine to their laundry to counteract the effects of silt as staff made the rounds of unoccupied rooms, flushing toilets to keep out brown water. Reaction to the inconvenience filled column after column in local newspapers. (Meanwhile, it's big news in the developing world if you can open your tap and drink from it.)

Even more dramatic are giant sinkholes, which open to swallow repair trucks, innocent civilians, and homes. The problems are especially severe in the Northeast and in older industrial cities, which rely on cast-iron mains installed in the early 1900s. Global warming is expected to bring more of these record-busting, pipe-bursting storms to wet regions of the world. (And perversely withhold rainfall in drier regions.)

Unless cities invest more to repair and replace their water and sewer systems, the EPA warns, nearly half of them will, by 2020, be in poor, very poor, or "life elapsed" status. The bill to take care of the drinking-water part, to hell with the sewers, will run $390 billion, according to the American Society of Civil Engineers.

Where will this money come from? Federal funds for drinking water and wastewater treatment are at their lowest level in a decade. Between 2001 and 2006, allocations declined from $1.3 billion to less than $900 million. "The Bush administration wants to phase out the state revolving fund for water," Nancy Stoner, director of the Natural Resources Defense Council's Clean Water Project, says. "They think it's a state and local issue." In 2003, the EPA estimated it would take nearly $277 billion to keep the nation's water-distribution systems up to par over the following twenty years.

In the feds' view, local utilities aren't charging enough for water. The government has a point: of all the developed nations, the United States pays the lowest tap-water rates, an average of $2.50 per thousand gallons. Sure, the rain and snow fall for free, but storing, treating, and distributing it aren't cheap, as just demonstrated. While some suggest a tax on bottled water or toilet paper (two cents a roll was the proposed rate in Florida), or the development of a trust fund supported by water polluters and industries that rely on clean water, the administration pins its hopes on "full cost pricing." In other words, raising the rates.

It's easy to scare up criticism of tap water—from environmental groups, academia, companies that sell bottled water and filters, and even from regulatory agencies that are supposed to be protecting water. Every time a town posts a boil-water alert, every time a well-water drinker shells out for tests and discovers something unsavory, every time a technician turns up an anomalous report or a water inspector gets caught fudging data (a criminal offense, but it's happened—in New York City, Philly, Boston, Providence, and Portland, Oregon), another tap-water drinker loses faith in the system. "It's always in the news—boil-water notices, bacteria alerts, notices in the mail," Cris Dockery, a co-owner of the Exell water company in Jackson, Mississippi, told the *Clarion-Ledger*. "The more and more that happens over a period of time, people start migrating toward what they trust, and they trust bottled water."

After learning about all the things that can go wrong with tap water, I don't know what to think, or drink. It would be easier if I fell into an obvious risk category: then I'd buy a super-duper filter and maintain it in a way that would make Mike Klender proud. Switching to bottled water isn't something I'm willing to contemplate at this point: it's expensive, it's heavy to haul around, and the production and disposal of all those bottles can't be good for the planet. Moreover, I'm coming to realize that when the commons—which include clean water and clean air—are either scarce or threatened, public authorities must manage them, and to do that they need our financial and moral support. Opting out of public water in favor of private isn't going to help preserve—or improve—municipal water supplies, but preserve them we must: too many people can afford to drink nothing but.

Of course, to feel truly comfortable with this decision I need to learn more about what comes out of my tap: I need to look beyond my annual report. But before I can arrange for a test, I notice something weird is happening with bottled water. Around the world, folks are starting to ask if it's really such a good idea.

Chapter 7

BACKLASH

IN THE SPRING of 2007, monster rainstorms lash Central Texas, leaving thousands of people without clean water. In June and July, it's the United Kingdom's turn: back-to-back-to-back storms leave 350,000 people in Gloucestershire and the surrounding region without sanitary services or drinking water. The normally terrible weather, locals say, has gotten worse. Next up is South Asia, where unremitting rains—their intensity unusual even for Nepal, India, and Pakistan—leave millions without water and other basics. Authorities send out boil-water alerts, and shoppers lucky enough to have a bottled-water aisle—and the money to make use of it—strip those aisles clean.

Meanwhile, the beverage industry continues to release sunny news: Americans bought nearly eleven billion dollars' worth of bottled water in 2006, and sales in 2007 are expected to rise 10 percent. In the European Union, South America, and Asia, the prognosis is similarly bright. I'm not surprised when I learn bad weather and good sales are linked.

But there are rumblings against bottled water too, and it isn't just the nuns and the communists this time. In March, Alice

Waters, goddess of the local-foods movement, decides to strike bottled water from her menu at Chez Panisse. "We asked where does all that energy and waste go, getting it to here and from here," Mike Kossa-Rienzi, the restaurant's general manager, says. "It wasn't a hard decision."

Soon, more restaurants on both U.S. coasts get religion. In London, where the distance food travels from farm to fork is already an obsession, the Green Party asks diners to request tap water; in France, fashion designer Pierre Cardin designs a water carafe, which he distributes free to thirty thousand Parisian restaurants, hoping to persuade his bottle-loving countrymen to drink from the tap (a mélange of groundwater from sixty-three springs, plus surface water from the Seine, Oise, and Marne rivers).

In San Francisco, which drinks EPA-approved unfiltered water from the Hetch Hetchy Reservoir, Mayor Gavin Newsom announces he'll no longer spend taxpayer dollars on bottled water—a savings of half a million dollars a year, not counting the cost of hauling the empties away. Mayors of Salt Lake City, Ann Arbor, Los Angeles, Santa Barbara, Santa Fe, and Minneapolis soon follow suit. New York City launches a seven-hundred-thousand-dollar ad campaign to promote tap, and Chicago passes a five-cent bottled-water tax, which is expected to raise more than ten million dollars a year for the city and also cut its waste-hauling costs (that is, if the law isn't overturned by angry retailers and the International Bottled Water Association, which represents 162 bottlers in the United States).

Suddenly bottled water is big news. Every time I open a newspaper, magazine, or Web browser, there's another story announcing that this harmless indulgence is anything but. On the lookout for this sort of material, I nearly drown in the tidal wave of eco-criticism. With a mounting sense of anticipation—how far will the attacks go, and is the backlash only a fad?—I watch as reporters, using statistics from academics and environmental groups, blast away at the bottled-water industry. But curiously, their focus isn't water, at first. It's oil.

Specifically, the seventeen million barrels it takes each year to make water bottles for the U.S. market. (Plastic-making also generates emissions of nickel, ethylbenzene, ethylene oxide, and benzene, but because we're in the thick of the global-warming movement, not the environmental-carcinogen movement, this doesn't get much play.) That's enough oil to fuel 1.3 million cars for a year.

Is seventeen million barrels a lot? Yes and no. Total U.S. oil consumption is twenty million barrels a *day*. But the small puddle that goes into polyethylene terephthalate doesn't include the energy needed to fill the bottles or to move them to consumers. Every week, a billion bottles snake through the country on tens of thousands of trucks, trains, and ships. (In 2007, Poland Spring alone burned 928,226 gallons of diesel fuel.) And then there's the energy it takes to chill water in fridges and to haul the empties off to landfills. It adds up.

Peter Gleick of the Pacific Institute estimates that the total energy required for every bottle's production, transport, and disposal is equivalent, on average, to filling that bottle a quarter of the way with oil. His finding, undisputed by the water-bottling industry, shocks me. (And yes, I realize that thicker plastic containers contain even more oil, but your average

American doesn't consume more than twenty gallons of, say, ketchup a year.) Oil, as we know, is a nonrenewable resource, mostly imported. The hunt for more oil is politically dangerous, scarily expensive, and environmentally ruinous.

And then there's the water itself—increasingly important as we enter what's been called the post–Peak Water era. Manufacturing and filling plastic water bottles consumes twice as much water as the bottle will ultimately contain, in part because bottle-making machines are cooled by water. Plants that use reverse osmosis to purify tap water lose between three and nine gallons of water—depending on how new the filters are and what they remove—for every filtered gallon that ends up on the shelf. Cleaning a bottling plant also requires a great deal of municipal water, especially if the end product is flavored. On average, only 60 to 70 percent of the water used by bottling plants ends up on supermarket shelves: the rest is waste.

Of course, all these costs—water, energy, oil—aren't unique to bottled water. It takes forty-eight gallons of water to make a gallon of beer, four gallons of water to make one of soda. Even a cow has a water footprint, drinking four gallons of water to produce one gallon of milk. But those other beverages aren't redundant to the calorie-free (and caffeine- and coloring-free) liquid that comes out of the tap, and that's an important distinction.

College lets out for the summer, and battalions of youthful volunteers from the noisy pressure group Corporate Accountability International (CAI) start hanging banners in public plazas across the nation. They fill plastic cups with water and invite open-minded passersby to take the Tap Water Challenge. More often than not, sippers can't differentiate between bottled water and tap. That's the first step in CAI's campaign to wean Americans from the bottle. But taste isn't everything, I'm learning. There's also the question of health.

After saying good-bye to Michael Mascha in Bryant Park, I cap my bottle of Singaporean NEWater and, back home, send its last few ounces to a water-testing lab. There isn't enough to run every assay, but I'm most interested in the nitrate level. Nitrate, remember, is colorless, odorless, and tasteless. It gets into drinking water from fertilizer and from animal and human waste. NEWater is, of course, made almost exclusively of the latter.

Rose, at the testing lab in Cleveland, isn't fazed to learn the provenance of my water, but she explains that the sample will be technically invalid, because it's more than a week old and hasn't been kept on bacteria-inhibiting ice. I tell her it's all the NEWater I've got and recite my credit-card number. When the results arrive in two weeks, I'm pleasantly surprised. Levels of metals and volatile organic compounds, including disinfection by-products, fall within safe ranges. And nitrate is only 2.8 parts per million—far less than Perrier's 18 ppm (or the EPA limit of 10). I want to call Mascha to gloat, but restrain myself.

Every now and then, academic scientists, environmental groups, or a municipality with something to prove decide to test the quality of bottled water, which, boasting of purity and healthfulness (or, in NEWater's case, its incontrovertible sustainability) seems to invite vicious attack. Inevitably, the testers report flaws. (If they don't come up with flaws, we don't hear the news: too dog-bites-man.)

The granddaddy of all bottled-water tests, if only for the amount of publicity it received, was performed in 1998 by the Natural Resources Defense Council, which looked at a thousand samples of 103 different brands of bottled water. A third showed such contaminants as arsenic, bromine, and coliform bacteria. In some samples, arsenic and carcinogenic compounds (disinfection by-products, that is) exceeded either state or industry standards; in others, those contaminants were present but at levels that didn't set off alarm bells. (The bottled-water-industry-supported Drinking Water Research Foundation refutes many of the claims made by the NRDC report.) In 2004, the FDA ran its own tests and found perchlorate at 0.45 ppb and 0.56 ppb in two samples of springwater. The levels were below those set by the few states that have a standard (the feds don't), but even a hint of rocket fuel, it's safe to say, isn't what consumers of springwater are expecting.

Arsenic is another story. When the FDA found 454 to 674 parts per billion in Jermuk water, from Armenia, it halted imports (the EPA and FDA limit is 10 ppb). The brand's die-hard Armenian-American fans were furious: "We've been drinking it all our life," they said. "It's a little piece of home."

In 1994, the Kansas Department of Health and Environment tested eighty brands of bottled water and found that at least 15 percent contained phthalates, a softening agent used in plastics, in amounts that exceeded federal standards; more than half contained the disinfection by-product chloroform, and slightly less than half contained bromodichloromethane—also a disinfection by-product. Twenty-five contained arsenic, fifteen contained lead, and nineteen had selenium, a trace mineral that, like many, is toxic in large amounts but beneficial in small. None of the chemicals presented an acute health risk.

In 2000, a peer-reviewed university study compared fifty-seven samples of bottled water to Cleveland tap and found more than a dozen had at least ten times the bacterial levels found in the city's water. (It is possible that the water started with a low count but the numbers went up as microorganisms happily multiplied in the warmth of closed containers.) A 2000 study by the Consumers Union confirmed what the NRDC had discovered: some brands had elevated bacterial counts. In 2004, the American Society of Microbiology tested sixty-eight types of mineral water and found that 40 percent contained bacteria or fungi, while twenty-one samples could support bacterial growth in lab cultures. Dangerous bacteria? Not necessarily: all the samples were safe to drink under government standards. If you are healthy, that is. The young, the old, and the otherwise infirm are warned to steer clear of such risks.

The message from water testers is loud and clear. Most bottled water is safe, by government standards. Almost always, the FDA sets levels for chemical, microbial, and radiological contaminants no less stringent than those of the EPA. It sounds good, but if you think you are buying pure, natural water from a pristine fount—and why wouldn't you, based on the labels' pretty pictures and on the amount of money you spent?—you might be disappointed to learn the FDA allows in bottled water the same complement of disinfection by-products, pesticides, heavy metals, and radioactive materials the EPA allows in tap. The only difference is that public water utilities are required in their annual reports to let you know, while the bottled-water industry has spent millions to make sure you don't, lobbying hard to keep such information off its labels.

Until recently, bottled water didn't contain fluoride—a selling point for many consumers wary of the compound. Now, however, some dentists worry that children who drink only bottled water are at risk for cavities. In response, a few bottlers have added fluoride to their products and marketed them to children. Nationwide, 67 percent of the population drinks from a fluoridated water supply, but the trend seems to be shifting away from the practice (most of Europe doesn't fluoridate, yet it's seen a sharp reduction in cavities). Some people consider fluoridation mass medicalization and the compound toxic (which it is, in doses far higher than what utilities serve up). The American Dental Association wants us to use fluoride (unless we're younger than two), but acknowledges we can get it from toothpaste, mouth rinse, fluoride supplements, and biannual fluoride treatments.

Another difference between bottled and tap: the EPA requires public water supplies to be disinfected and tested for crypto, giardia, and viruses. But because springwater comes from underground and isn't expected to harbor those organisms, the FDA doesn't require bottlers to test for them. ("Purified water," of course, starts from the tap, so it's already assumed to have met EPA standards.) And just because bottling companies have fancy filtration equipment doesn't mean they maintain it; dirty filters can put schmutz into water, instead of removing it.

While utilities test tap water hundreds of thousands of times a year and report their results to state and federal agencies, bottling plants self-test (Nestlé claims to test one hundred times a day; DS Waters, the biggest home-and-office water-delivery company in the nation, tests four times a year), and they host an FDA inspector infrequently. The plants have low priority, says the agency, because the industry has a good safety record. When inspectors do show up, they test only for selected contaminants, depending on the reason for the sampling. A scolding July 2007 report on general food safety by the House Energy and Commerce Committee states, "FDA has no rules governing testing protocols, record retention . . . manufacturing, quality assurance and control, or the right to examine any records that a food-processing firm chooses to keep voluntarily." According to William K. Hubbard, a former FDA assistant commissioner, most domestic plants are inspected only once every five to ten years.

And then there's this: if bottled water is packaged and sold within the same state, it's exempt from regulation by the FDA. But that hardly ever happens, says Joseph Doss, president of the International Bottled Water Association (IBWA), "because the bottle, the label, and the cap all have to come from the same state." He can't tell me which bottlers fit these criteria. If a bottler is exempt from FDA oversight, it is subject to state standards, which vary widely in rigor and scope. Roughly one in five states has no bottled-water standards at all. Luckily, the IBWA subjects its members to annual surprise inspections and stricter health standards. For example, IBWA has zero tolerance for fecal coliform (unlike the FDA). Unfortunately, its standards aren't legally binding or enforceable, not every bottler is a member (Nestlé is; Coke and Pepsi aren't), and consumers have no way of learning the results of inspections.

When a lot of people get sick from tap water, the public hears about it. The reporting system for bottled water is more porous. There have been no confirmed cases of illness from drinking bottled water in the United States (though there have been about a hundred recalls here, and plenty of reports of illness associated with bottled water in Africa, Asia, and Europe). Either it hasn't happened in the U.S., it hasn't been reported to the public, or it's happened but the source of the illness wasn't successfully traced. If there is a recall, the news often arrives late. A report from the Worldwatch Institute notes, "in most cases the products may be recalled up to 15 months after the problematic water was produced, distributed, and sold."

Problematic water doesn't always, or even often, send you rushing to the bathroom, let alone to your gastroenterologist. But its consequences can be worse, over the long haul. In 2006, springwater produced in and sold throughout western New York State was found to contain up to twenty-five parts per billion of the carcinogen bromate, a level two and a half times higher than the EPA limit. (Bromate is formed when bromide, which is naturally occurring and harmless, meets ozone during purification.) The industry cited the subsequent recall as proof that the system works. Those who drank dangerous levels of bromate for well over a month probably feel differently.

The Poland Spring bottling plant in Hollis, Maine, fills between five and six million bottles a day, 358 days a year. A $240 million affirmation of market trends, it's the largest such plant in North America. Tom Brennan and Bill Maples, its manager, invite me to take a look around, but first they get me to put on a hairnet, safety glasses, and earplugs. Now I look like an alien too.

Emerging through double doors onto the production floor, I need a few moments to get my bearings. Almost everything seems to be in motion: small plastic tubes called preforms glide along overhead "airveyor" belts. Blasts of air expand them into half-liter bottles, which dangle from their necks like chickens in a processing plant. Three lines of empties swerve and merge into a single stream. "Powered by air," Maples yells over the roar, all pride.

Inside a small, glass-walled room under positive air pressure, one machine fills the bottles and another caps them, twelve hundred per minute. Turning a corner, I smell melting plastic—"That's the laser, etching on codes," Maples says. Working at blur speed, machines slap on the famous green label, corral bottles into cases, wrap cases in polyethylene film. Humans take over from here, stacking the cases five feet high.

I take a moment to drink it all in and ask Maples how many bottles we're contemplating. "Twenty-five million," he says, gesturing to the canyon of water that covers six acres of the plant's floor. It will be gone in less than a week, replaced by twenty-five million bottles more.

Before leaving, I take a quick look inside the lab, where technicians continuously test samples from various points along the production line and run hourly samples of the finished product, screening for more than two hundred contaminants annually. Nestlé reports all this information on its Web site, but again, this is self-reporting, and the information, when I check it, is a year out-of-date. Still, I give the company credit for trying.

Sometimes, when testers take a close look at bottled water that may be up to two years old, they find contaminants that got an ND (for "not detected" at or above the minimum reporting level) when the company ran its own analyses. These contaminants have nothing to do with the water itself: they come from its plastic packaging.

Most water bottles are made from polyethylene terephthalate (PET), a polymer derived from oil, with other ingredients added for flexibility, color, and strength. I keep hearing about a softening agent, called phthalates, used to make some plastics flexible. I keep hearing, also, that they're known to disrupt the endocrine system, ever so important in growth and development. In 2005, the European Union banned the use of six different phthalates in toys and child-care articles; in 2007, California followed suit. Neither PET nor bottle caps made of polypropylene contain phthalates, but those cloudy white water jugs made of high-density polyethylene (HDPE)—the big ones with the built-in spigot and the one-gallon jugs—do. The EPA regulates phthalates in tap water, but the FDA, lobbied by the bottled-water industry, refused to do so until the late nineties. The IBWA's phthalate limits match the EPA's, though it measures levels at the plant, not in water that has been stored for months or even years.

What about those other ingredients in plastic bottles? In 2006, William Shotyk, a geochemist at the University of Heidelberg, found antimony, used as a catalyst in the manufacture of PET, leaching into bottled water. Ingested in small doses antimony can cause dizziness and depression; in large doses, nausea, vomiting, and death. The amounts Shotyk detected were well below government standards, but they kept rising the longer water stayed in PET containers. Samples opened immediately after bottling had 160 parts per trillion (the U.S. allows 6 parts per billion, equivalent to 6,000 parts per trillion, in tap water). After three months, the antimony level doubled, and after another three months it nearly doubled again. Still, it was well below federal limits.

And the effects of extreme temperatures on water bottles? An Internet rumor warns that freezing releases scary chemicals, such as dioxin, into your water. False: if anything, cooling slows down the migration of chemicals. Besides, PET doesn't contain dioxin—the carcinogen is generated only at temperatures above seven hundred degrees, a temperature the interior of your car is unlikely to reach, even with the windows rolled up in Death Valley in August.

The FDA insists PET plastic is safe for food products, under normal conditions (don't microwave it). But the agency stops short of saying chemicals don't leach into food and water. Instead, it says levels of chemical migration from PET bottles are "well within the margin of safety based on information available to the agency." It isn't a ringing endorsement, especially since manufacturers themselves supply the information to the FDA, and science continues to find evidence that chemicals can have negative health effects at levels well below those approved for everyday use.

After leaving the Hollis plant I drive up to the Poland Spring museum, in the company's Preservation Park, in Poland. Alone in the original bottling plant, now renovated as a stately visitors' center, I wander past science displays and Poland Spring memorabilia. Inside a diorama, a mannequin in a lab coat—with his thick, dark wig, push-broom mustache, and wire-rimmed glasses, he resembles George Harrison—gazes soulfully at nineteenth-century water-testing equipment. Contemplating him, I try to imagine what it was like in the pre-chlorination days to live in mortal fear of raw water (as do billions in the developing world today). From fear to fashion, I think, as I review bottled water's timeline, from therapeutic treatments for visiting dignitaries to status symbol for social climbers to product placement on TV dramas. It remains to be seen how, or if, the Poland Spring museum addresses the current mood of bottled-water skepticism.

I have to say, after my tap-water investigations, that I'm not immune to the appeal of springwater. The major brands come from reasonably protected sources, they contain no chlorination by-products, and they're more or less a natural product—a far cry from big-city municipal water. Al Gore requested springwater—a regional brand, "not Evian"—when he toured with *An Inconvenient Truth*. (And when he went to the Academy Awards he drank Biota, the official water of the Oscars, which came in a bottle made from corn. The company, which drew water from springs in Ouray, Colorado, filed for bankruptcy shortly after its star turn: too much biota—plant and animal life—in the water.)

In a trance induced by the sounds of plashing water, I make my way to a cooler filled with company product. PLEASE DO NOT REFILL WATER BOTTLES reads a small sign. The spell is broken and, annoyed by Nestlé's greediness, I top off my reusable from the spigot. Is it dangerous to refill a PET bottle? Or are the bottlers merely pushing us to buy more water? Refilling a PET bottle, I learn, is dangerous only if harmful bacteria have grown inside it. If you have the time and fortitude to wash your bottle with warm, soapy water (a bottle brush is handy), more power to you. Me, I'll stick with my widemouthed Nalgene.

But not with complete confidence. Hard polycarbonate bottles, some with the resin code 7 on the bottom, seem like the ultimate reusable: easy to wash, hard to shatter. But polycarbonate is now known to leach tiny amounts of bisphenol A (BPA), a chemical that mimics estrogen. (The more scratched your bottle, and the hotter the liquid inside it, the more it leaches.) A study by the Centers for Disease Control and Prevention found BPA in 95 percent of the people who were tested at levels at or above those that affected development in animals. Everyone, it seems, has had chronic, low-level exposure. BPA comes from those five-gallon water jugs used for home and office delivery, from baby bottles, the linings of food cans, dental sealants, and some wine vats, water mains, and tanks lined with epoxy resins.

According to more than a hundred government-funded studies, tiny amounts of BPA cause genetic changes that lead to prostate cancer, as well as decreased testosterone, low sperm counts, and signs of early female puberty in lab animals. The genetic mechanisms affected by these chemicals work similarly in all animals—including humans. A review conducted by the National Institutes of Health concluded BPA does pose some human health risks to fetuses and children, though they were mostly classified as minimal. The makers and users of BPA say the chemical poses no risk to humans, but their studies looked at high doses, not low (yes, it's counterintuitive, but studies show tiny amounts have negative effects not always seen at higher levels). The IBWA isn't concerned with bisphenol and doesn't test for it.

A direct connection between BPA and human illness has yet to be proved. But Patricia Hunt, a molecular biologist at Case Western Reserve University who's been studying the chemical for nearly a decade, says, "If we wait for comparable human data and it comes out like animal data, we aren't going to be breeding as a species."

And that's enough for me. I toss my oldest Nalgenes and buy a couple of Sigg bottles, made of aluminum and lined with a water-based nontoxic polymer, so far unindicted by the chemical police. Here, finally, is a clear-cut step I can take to protect my family and myself from the modern world. I'm still not over the shock of learning what's sometimes in tap water (even if it occurs at levels acceptable to the government), but at least it's not growing bacteria, thanks to the chlorine; it's not laced with plastic by-products, like water that's been sitting on a shelf for months; it's closely monitored; it has a relatively small carbon footprint; and I'm not paying a private company exorbitant amounts to deliver it.

The summer grinds on, the Corporate Accountability volunteers run their taste tests, and the media continue to link bottled water with global warming. No bottler is hit harder in the great carbon dustup than Fiji Water. The number two imported brand in the United States, after Evian, Fiji is pumped from an aquifer beneath a "pristine" rain forest on Viti Levu—more than a million bottles of it a day—then shipped to the United States and other ports. The company, owned by Roll International, trades on its distance from industry and pollution: remoteness makes its water "more pure" and "healthier than other bottled waters." But that distance—more than five thousand miles to the port of San Francisco, where it is loaded onto trucks and trains for delivery to zip codes from coast to coast—has another dimension. According to the Natural Resources Defense Council, shipping a million gallons of water from Fiji to New York City generates 190 tons of carbon dioxide. (The average American generates more than 20 tons of carbon dioxide per year.)

There's another environmental cost to Fiji Water: the bottling plant, in need of a steady power source, runs three diesel generators twenty-four hours a day. Charles Fishman writes, in *Fast Company* magazine, "The water may come from 'one of the last pristine ecosystems on earth,' as some of the labels say, but out back of the bottling plant is a less pristine ecosystem veiled with a diesel haze."

Away from the rain forest, Fiji's urban areas are chronically water-stressed—not because there isn't enough water around, but because the infrastructure to deliver and protect it is inadequate. "The population is growing, and there isn't proper planning or pumping stations," a functionary at the Fijian embassy in New York tells me. (Embassy employees drink neither from the tap nor from Fiji bottles but from a Poland Spring cooler.) In 2007, half the nation didn't have access to clean water. Flash floods during the rainy season lead to outbreaks of typhoid, leptospirosis, and dengue fever. During these events, Fijians are advised to boil their water or drink from the bottle.

It makes a neat story for the antibottle crowd. Water is sent thousands of miles to people who already have clean, cheap water (us), while locals at the source go thirsty. But will boycotting Fiji Water help the Fijians? No, and there's evidence it would actually cause hardship. Roll has reinvested all its profits since 2004 into the business and the island. It built schools for its workers' children and puts money into a trust for water infrastructure. The company employs more than three hundred Fijians, paying them twice the informal minimum wage. Boycott Fiji Water and a burgeoning local economy will falter, even as the air quality near the plant—and everywhere Fiji's ships and trucks roam—improves. In Fiji, as in Fryeburg, nothing's simple.

The mayors who canceled their bottled-water contracts in the summer of 2007 burnished their eco-cred, but their primary motivation may have been fiscal. Buying water is expensive; so is collecting bottles and delivering them to dumps. Most U.S. communities can recycle the empties, but because most bottled water is consumed in places that often lack recycling bins—on the street, in movie theaters, at parks, and on the road—the product has a pitiful recovery rate: barely 15 percent. Most single-serve bottles are either buried in landfills or burned in incinerators, or they make their way to the far corners of the earth: blown underneath train platforms, into the back of caves and alleys, along roadways, onto beaches, and out to the middle of the ocean, where the containers break into tiny pieces that sea creatures mistake for food.

As the prices of oil and natural gas rise, plastic becomes more valuable. Processors in the United States are desperate to get their hands on more PET. In 2007, recyclers sold the commodity for between forty-six and fifty-four cents a pound. Still, end users in China are willing to offer more, and so about 40 percent of the plastic collected for recycling in the States makes its way overseas.

Whether here or there, the bottles are chopped into flakes, then turned into pea-size pellets that can be extruded to make fibers for clothing, carpeting, strapping, and other products. Recycling our bottles is better than trashing them, because it reduces the demand for landfill space, but it isn't greatly reducing U.S. water bottlers' demand for oil because most of them aren't using recycled content.

"There are taste issues with it," Ron Dyer, an environmental manager at Nestlé Waters, tells me.

"Getting enough of it is a problem," Stephen Mahabir, plant manager at the Dasani plant in Queens, New York, says. Which is it? I phone Betty McLaughlin, executive director of the Container Recycling Institute.

"The bottlers might be wary of being asked to help pay for recycling programs if they started to use significant amounts of recycled content," she says. That, plus virgin PET costs less than recycled PET.

McLaughlin's group promotes bottle bills, which require consumers to pay a refundable deposit on beverage containers. Eleven states have such laws for soft drinks and beer, but only three apply the law to water (until January of 2009, that is, when Oregon will become the fourth state). Do bottle bills work? Yes. States with them recycle 60 to 90 percent of their beverage containers, versus a national average of 23 percent for states without. In New York City, where I live, we have a curbside program for narrow-necked plastic containers, and a bottle bill for carbonated drinks. If the state expanded that bill to cover water and upped the deposit from a nickel to a dime, it's doubtful our streets and parks would be saturated with empty water bottles.

Not surprisingly, bottlers don't like such bills: the programs cost them a penny or two per container (after scrap revenue and unclaimed deposits are figured in, says the Container Recycling Institute), and they create headaches for grocers who handle all those empties. Every time a new bottle bill, or the expansion of an existing bill, makes it to a state legislature, Coke, Pepsi, and other bottlers hire lobbyists and run ad campaigns designed to stop them. And they usually do.

In a landfill, heavy equipment crushes water bottles, but they still take up space. For how long? No one knows: after all, PET is only about twenty-five years old. But estimates range up to a thousand years. Are the bottles leaching toxins in there? Possibly phthalates from the HDPE jugs, and possibly benzene, nickel, and the ethylenes from other types of plastic. It's hard to be certain since no one has ponied up funding to pinpoint the sources of these contaminants in landfill leachate.

In incinerators, PET bottles generate about eleven thousand BTUs per pound of bottles—good news for anyone harnessing energy from combustion. But since it takes about forty-nine thousand BTUs to *produce* one pound of PET, burning it for fuel is plain silly. Incinerating PET also contributes to the formation of polyaromatic hydrocarbons (PAHs), which sound nice but can—some of them—be carcinogenic and bioaccumulative (that is, they build up in the tissues of living organisms). PAHs produced in incinerators end up in stack gases (which drift into the jet stream), in bottom ash, and in the residue collected by sophisticated scrubbers. The same goes for the heavy metal antimony. And where do these sequestered pollutants end up? Usually in landfills.

No one uses more plastic water bottles than Pepsi, which makes the bestselling Aquafina. But it doesn't fill those bottles close to my home, so I start phoning a plant in Queens that produces the number-two-selling purified water, Dasani. It takes me four months to arrange a tour, but eventually I learn quite a bit about Coca-Cola's multistep filtering and that water quality is the least important factor in deciding where to locate a bottling facility. "The end product is the same at every plant," Stephen Mahabir says, sitting across from me at the plant's conference table, in the shadow of the Long Island Expressway. "You could take mud and end up with Dasani." My handler from the regional office, sitting next to me, gives Mahabir a penetrating look.

"How do you describe the taste of the finished product?" I ask.

In one voice, three Coke soldiers recite, "Crisp, refreshing."

Donning shower cap and earplugs, I race through the bottling plant with Mahabir, noting tanks, tubes, and pipes. He points out machines that subject the water to ultrafiltration and carbon filtration (to trap tiny organic and inorganic particles), to ultraviolet light (which inactivates cryptosporidium), and to reverse osmosis (which removes all traces of minerals and salts). I see the machine that injects the water with new minerals and salts, which give Dasani its distinctive taste, and the contraption that blasts the final product with disinfecting ozone.

When my allotted time is up, I've got more questions. Over the next week, I phone and e-mail the regional handler, who eventually concedes I must call HQ, in Atlanta. But when I telephone and e-mail my queries to the next gatekeeper— questions about water use, recycling, and bottle bills—I fall into a black hole.

Months pass, I repeat my inquiries, and suddenly Coke starts talking—not to me but to the world. The company is cutting water use, it announces, through reduction and reuse. (In 2006, Coke used 290 billion liters of water to produce 114 billion liters of beverages.) It plans to lightweight its Dasani bottles, from 18.2 grams of plastic to 13.8. It's going to build a plant in Spartanburg, South Carolina, and recycle as many as two billion bottles a year, producing about one hundred million pounds of food-grade recycled PET each year. (In 2006, almost four *billion* pounds of PET were trashed—equivalent to roughly seventy-two billion bottles.) Whether the company will use that PET in its own bottles remains to be seen.

I'd love to take credit for inspiring the company's actions, but my handlers never returned my calls. Had they, I could have reminded them that waste activists still mistrust Coke for backing down on a 2003 pledge to use 10 percent recycled content by 2005. (In 2006, according to the trade journal *Plastic News*, the company used just 3.8 percent recycled content in its soda bottles; in 2005, Pepsi used 10 percent in its soda bottles.) I would have said that setting up a recycling plant is good, but it hardly makes up for the fact the company is still producing and selling, for enormous profit, unhealthy drinks (sodas, that is). And that while recycling is virtuous, it is less environmentally preferable to reusing and refilling bottles.

Coke isn't the only company scrutinizing its environmental footprint in this summer of discontent. Pulled by economics (waste is expensive) and pushed by activists (expert at embarrassing industry for its excesses), other bottlers start announcing changes as well. Nestlé shrinks its cardboard packaging, reduces the weight of its bottles from 15 to 12.5 grams of plastic, cuts the area of its paper labels by 30 percent, inaugurates a recycling program at the New York Marathon (where seventy-five thousand one-gallon Poland Spring containers water the runners), starts pushing a variety of stakeholders to develop a comprehensive redemption system for plastic packaging (a huge breakthrough, if it works), slashes water use to the lowest in the industry, and converts sixty-four tanker trucks to run on a biodiesel mixture made from rendered animal fat and soy. The switch will reduce the fleet's carbon emissions by more than 1.8 million pounds per year. "I'm pretty sure we'll score an A," Kim Jeffery, chief of Nestlé Waters North America, tells the *New York Times* in an article about downsized packaging. "Let's see if it translates into more business."

Still, Nestlé has some stiff competition in Icelandic Glacial. In June of 2007, that company goes carbon neutral: its plant in Thorlakshofn runs on hydroelectric power, and the company buys carbon offsets to absolve its greenhouse sin of shipping (but not trucking). Allen Hershkowitz, of the Natural Resources

Defense Council, notes the irony of bottles that depict snow-capped mountains and glaciers "when in fact the production of the bottle is contributing to global warming, which is melting those snowcaps and those glaciers."

Months later, Fiji Water snatches back the spotlight by going "carbon negative," installing a windmill to power its plant, switching to biodiesel and other alternative fuels for its trucks, and buying carbon offsets to cover emissions it cannot eliminate.

Perhaps the biggest victory for critics of the bottled-water industry is Pepsi's decision, under pressure from Corporate Accountability International, to spell out PUBLIC WATER SUPPLY on its Aquafina labels (the ersatz mountain picture, however, will stay). "This is a huge first step on the way to stop branding water in a way that undermines confidence in tap water," Mark Hays, a senior researcher with the group, says. The online community and the print media take merciless potshots at Pepsi for making huge profits off tap water, and Pepsi responds with ads that tout its seven-step purification process.

Every time I hear about Coke or Pepsi's elaborate filtration procedure, I sink a little deeper into a funk. Why is there so much stuff to remove from tap water? Because we've neglected our pipes and conduits, I remind myself; we've washed drugs and industrial and agriculture contaminants into our rivers; we've condoned urban sprawl, which sends sediment, upon which bacteria thrive, into our reservoirs; and our efforts at disinfection sometimes make matters worse.

The alternative—bottled water—presents another set of issues. Producing and transporting it burns oil, which contributes to global warming, and the bottles themselves may harm our health by leaching chemicals. As we hurtle into the future, all of our drinking-water choices seem to be problematic. If only we'd taken better care of our resources yesterday, we wouldn't be in this mess today. And while my first instinct is to blame the government for letting agriculture, industry, and developers off the hook, I have to admit it's all of us: it's the way we've come to live. We want convenience, cheap food, a drug for every mood, bigger houses, and faster gadgets. Whether it's building a second home or manufacturing meat, magazines, or mopeds, it all takes a toll on our water.

The bottled-water backlash, combined with dire predictions of worldwide water shortages and their attendant human misery, bring water charities out of the woodwork. Give us your money, their full-page ads say, and we'll dig wells and lay pipe for the thirsty poor. All kinds of celebrities, including Madonna (who did so much for sales of Evian in a more innocent time), lend their names and images to the cause of water for the people: The Tap Project, Blue Planet Run, Global Green, H2O Africa. (Deaf to the clamor, Jennifer Aniston goes the other way, signing a contract to endorse Smartwater. Some ads depict her naked and others place her, clad, in an elegant restaurant, where her plastic water bottle looks, to someone with my peculiar mindset, like litter amid the crystal stemware.)

Are the water projects worthwhile? "It's that old distinction between doing good and making change—the latter is a matter of policy and organizing and rights," Alan Snitow, coauthor with Deborah Kaufman and Michael Fox, of *Thirst: Fighting the*

Corporate Theft of Our Water, writes to me. "The former is a matter of money and largesse that usually redounds to the benefit (or image) of the donor more than changing the long-term situation of recipients."

Competing in a supercrowded field for limited consumer dollars, some water bottlers start to connect the dots. Eschewing appeals to wellness, they play to social conscience: choose our product, and we'll send a portion of profits to a watery cause. Starbucks was an early adopter. It sells Ethos water, for $1.80 per half liter, with the copy line "Every bottle makes a difference." How much of a difference? A nickel for every bottle, up to $10 million over five years, goes to nonprofits that focus on water delivery, sanitation, and hygiene. To reach the goal of $10 million, Starbucks will have to sell forty million bottles of water a year—water trucked from springs in Baxter, California, and Hazleton, Pennsylvania—leaving behind $350 million in revenue when all is said and done.

Conscientious Canadians can buy Earth Water, which comes from the city of Edmonton's municipal supply, and support the United Nations' water work. In the eastern United States there's Keeper Springs, founded by Robert F. Kennedy Jr. and Chris Bartle, a sustainable-business entrepreneur. Keeper Springs is bottled in Vermont, has minuscule distribution in New York and New England, and funnels all its after-tax profits to the Waterkeeper Alliance. (There aren't many: in 2006, the company sold only 130,000 cases of water—about 55,000 less than what Poland Spring's Hollis plant produces in a day.)

Why, I ask Bartle, would a group focused on protecting public waterways and municipal supplies promote the purchase of private water? "I want to put it right up there on the Web site," Bartle says. " 'We advise you not to buy our product. We advise you to drink tap water.' " But he doesn't think the convenience-minded public will listen. (After our talk, the Web site changes to reflect his pro-tap ideas.) Bartle's point: if you must buy bottled water, buy ours. At least it will do some good.

That's what all the ethical waterists say.

In Britain, the socially conscious can buy Thirsty Planet or Belu, which funnel money through water charities to Africa. Both companies trade on awareness of water equity, but Belu scores some environmental points too. The company uses wind energy, offsets its carbon dioxide emissions by funding clean-energy projects, and uses bottles made, in the United States, of corn.

(A few words about corn plastic: its manufacture generates fewer greenhouse gases than plastic made from oil, and yes, corn is a renewable, instead of a fossil, resource. But corn is hardly sustainable, not the way it's grown in this country. Farmed at an industrial scale, corn requires vast amounts of herbicides and fertilizer. With heavy rain, these inputs run into waterways and pollute drinking water. Corn plastic is compostable, but only in a commercial operation: very few backyard bins or piles get hot enough for degradation to take place in a reasonable amount of time. If your community doesn't collect materials for composting, your bottle will likely end up in a landfill. Recyclers don't like corn plastic either: it doesn't mix well with the conventional stuff. Processors have to pay to sort it out, then pay again to dispose of it.)

Ethical waters make consumers feel good about buying

bottled water, but they have some insidious side effects. They undermine confidence in tap water, which may erode public support that's crucial for its upkeep and improvement; they do nothing to solve the problems that spur consumers to buy bottled water in the first place; they perpetuate the idea that water is a commodity; and they subtly make us forget that Starbucks, or any other food-service establishment, has a perfectly good spigot behind its counter.

But what if the water or pipes aren't perfectly good? There's a market opportunity here as well: the water filter, a natural middle ground in the battle between the bottle and the tap. By 2007, approximately 60 percent of U.S. households had some kind of water filtration system, up from 40 percent in 2000. Ads for refrigerators promote their built-in filters, and under-the-sink devices are suddenly part of real-estate advertising, one of the essential "mod cons." The U.S. market for residential water treatment was estimated, in 2006, to be worth $1.5 billion, and it's growing at an annual rate of between 9 and 11 percent.

I'm doing my part: I've got the Brita UltraMax perched atop my fridge, filtering the Catskills' and Delaware's finest. The leader in the "pour through" market, Brita's white-topped pitchers with the carbon filters can be found in 35 percent of American homes. Between 2002 and 2007, sales have been steady at about three million units a year.

Things are about to look even better for Brita (named after the German inventor's daughter). The bottle backlash, coupled with not-so-latent fears about what lurks in household pipes, gives the company a substantial bump. "The criticism *has* been good for business," Drew McGowan, a company spokesperson, tells me. Sales jump 11 percent in a single quarter. "Why should we waste money on bottled water? Tap is pretty good."

I remind McGowan that as recently as 2006, Brita ran ads in Canada and, before that, in the United States that slammed municipal supplies. "Obviously, that's not our marketing direction now," he says.

Brita's marketing direction now closely echoes that of bottled water, with an emphasis on health and wellness, for which the universal shorthand seems to be a beautiful woman in a yoga pose. Drink enough water, says Brita's Web site, and you'll take fewer trips to the dentist, your skin will glow, and you'll sleep better.

A week after I talk to McGowan, Brita develops an ethical component: buy one of their pitchers plus a Nalgene, and the companies will send some of the proceeds to the Blue Planet Run Foundation. It's a perfect lesson in capitalism: smart marketing persuaded us to buy bottled water in the first place; now that bottled water is a problem, smart marketing tells us to solve it by buying something else.

I did: I got those Siggs. So do many others. Between May and August, the Swiss company's sales shoot up 200 percent. Sigg's U.S. president, Steve Wasik, says the bottles—now in groovy patterns with slogans like "make love not landfill"— "are an accessory like your cell phone or your iPod."

The analogy makes perfect sense from a marketing point of view, but buying a refillable bottle is opposite to the hyperindividualism of buying a private phone or musical headset. Refillables announce a commitment to public water, a heartening step away from what Andrew Szasz, in *Shopping Our Way to Safety: How We Changed from Protecting the Environment to Protecting Our-selves*, has called the inverted quarantine, in which Americans remove themselves from environmental problems by buying things (fallout shelters, homes in suburbs, organic food, bottled water) instead of working on solutions through political orga-nizing. In the nineties, we started buying bottled water to pro-tect ourselves from tap (and to distinguish ourselves from the masses). Now, thanks to rising eco-consciousness, a segment of society is going in the other direction. If buying something new—a filter or bottle—makes this more palatable to the consumption-addled populace, so be it.

Using a pour-through filter is ten to twenty times cheaper than buying bottled water. But what does it actually do? Sylvie Chavanne, Brita's research-and-development group manager, explains that the filter contains charcoal, derived from either burnt coconut husks or coal, and ion-exchange beads, which are made of plastic resin, derived from oil.

"The charcoal pieces open and create pores," she says. "They have sites to which molecules want to attach." Mole-cules of chlorine, for example: Brita removes them all. Its ion-exchange beads are treated to bond with and reduce lead, foremost, followed by copper, cadmium, mercury, and benzene.

Chavanne stresses that a Brita improves drinking water—particularly its taste and odor—but it doesn't deal with catastrophic situations. Does a Brita remove traces of pharma-ceuticals? No, Chavanne says. Perchlorate? No. "We can't claim to take it out if we don't test for it, and we don't test for it if the EPA doesn't have a standard."

What about disinfection by-products? "Only benzene is reduced with the pour-through filter, but the on-tap filter removes trihalomethanes and a long list of volatile organic compounds." Phosphorus, nitrates, nitrogen? No. Fluoride? No. Sulfur? No. Arsenic? No. Iron? "We don't claim it, though the resin could attract it." She has no explanation for the brownish fuzz, which I diagnosed as iron oxide, on the bottom of my Brita tank.

How about bacteria or cysts? No—they are too small to be trapped by the charcoal, at least in the pour-through filter. "With the on-tap model," Chavanne says, "the carbon block is tight enough to exclude cysts. If it were that tight in the pour-through, water couldn't get through on gravity alone." (The PUR Plus filter, which sports a "pleated microfilter," claims to remove cysts of crypto and giardia; the regular filter reduces more or less the same contaminants as the Brita.)

Chlorine's yucky taste is the reason a lot of otherwise sane people drink bottled water. But removing chlorine doesn't require much equipment: all you have to do is let your water stand a few hours in an uncovered pitcher or jug.

"Does Brita's tight cover prevent chlorine from off-gassing?" I ask Chavanne.

"Hmm," she says, thinking. "If you fill your reservoir, in six minutes the water has filtered through. So the carbon would remove the chlorine."

"And without chlorine in the water, can the bacteria regrow?"

"Yes, if you leave your filtered water in the sun for days, you may see microorganisms appear. But it's the same with water that hasn't been through a Brita: there are organisms in the air, on our lips, and hands. If you use well water, God knows what's in *there*."

"So people with well water shouldn't rely on—" I was about to say charcoal filters, but Chavanne interrupts me.

"Their well!" She isn't against well water per se, it turns out, but she highly recommends that people with wells test their water. (Standard tests for microbes cost about sixty-five dollars; tests for pesticides and herbicides can bring the bill to well over four hundred dollars. Testing for all possible pollutants could run more than two grand.)

"Can Brita filters be recycled?" A quick calculation tells me Americans went through more than sixty million between 2002 and 2007. "In Europe, people return them to retailers, who return them to Brita," Chavanne says. The company segregates the carbon from the resin, then sells the charcoal for use in road construction. The resin beads are stripped of the metals they pulled from water and then processed into new beads. In the United States, of course, the culture of returning products to manufacturers is in its infancy. Brita did it for a while here, then lost its charcoal buyer. For now, the filters go in the trash.

As 2007 winds down, opposition to bottled water is still winding up. Going into autumn, sales have dropped only slightly, but it's hard to say if it's due to activist pressure, cool weather, high prices (oil costs more) or, as Nestlé's Kim Jeffery says, a lack of natural disasters, which always spur demand. Billions of cases of water continue to march out of supermarkets, and millions of bottles dribble from everyplace else.

"People don't go backwards," says Arthur Von Wiesen-berger, author of *The Pocket Guide to Bottled Water* and a consultant to the beverage industry. "Once they've developed a taste for bottled water, they won't give it up." Market analysts predict that bottled-water consumption and sales for 2007 will, when the final tallies are in, at least match the numbers from 2006; Fiji Water alone expects a 20 percent increase in exports in 2007. New bottling plants open in the United States, Europe, India, and Canada; entrepreneurs announce plans to bottle water in the Amazon, among other fragile landscapes, and Nestlé continues to buy and explore new spring sites.

Still, among a certain psychographic, bottled water is now the mark of the devil, the moral equivalent of driving a Hummer. No longer socially useful, it's shunned in many restaurants, where ordering tap is all the rage. Writing in *Slate*, Daniel Gross calls this new snob appeal entirely predictable. "So long as only a few people were drinking Evian, Perrier, and San Pellegrino, bottled water wasn't perceived as a societal ill. Now that everybody is toting bottles of Poland Spring, Aquafina, and Dasani, it's a big problem." By democratizing bottled water—lowering its price and broadening its target—commodity waters wrecked the party for everyone.

But is it fashion or is it a rising awareness of the bottle's environmental toll that's driving the backlash? I'm starting to think they're the same thing. Fashion drove a certain segment of society to embrace bottled water in the first place, and fashion (green chic, that is) may drive that same segment to reject it. But the imperative to stop global warming—the biggest reason for the backlash—reaches only so far. For some, the imperative to protect oneself from tap water that either tastes bad or *is* bad, or the simple allure of convenience, may trump any planetary concerns.

The International Bottled Water Association is counting on it. Now in panic mode, the group is deflecting critics left and right. Bottled water uses only 0.02 percent of the world's groundwater, Joseph Doss, the group's president, argues in full-page advertisements and in interviews with the media. (Yes, but it takes all those gallons from just a few places.) Other beverages move around the country, and the world, too: it's unfair to single out bottled water for opprobrium. (True: only about 10 percent of bottled water, by volume, is imported in the United States, compared with 25 to 30 percent of wine. But we don't drink twenty-eight gallons of wine per person per year, and wine doesn't, alas, flow from our taps.)

Bottled water is a healthy alternative to high-calorie drinks, says the IBWA: it competes with soda, not tap. "Any efforts to discourage water consumption are not in the public's interest," Doss says. (What a difference seven years make: in 2000, Robert S. Morrison, then CEO of Quaker Oats, soon to merge with PepsiCo, told a reporter, "The biggest enemy is tap water." And Susan D. Wellington, vice president of marketing for Gatorade, owned by Pepsi, said to a group of New York analysts, "When we're done, tap water will be relegated to showers and washing dishes." In 2006, Fiji Water took that dig at Cleveland, with its "The Label Says Fiji Because It's Not Bottled in Cleveland" ad.)

Since Americans still drink almost twice as much soda as bottled water, it's not surprising that Coca-Cola, owner of Vitaminwater, and PepsiCo. are covering all their bases. The companies now offer vitamin-fortified *sodas*, extending what Michael Pollan calls "the Wonder bread strategy of supplementation to junk food in its purest form."

The bottling industry also plays the emergency card: consumers should consider bottled water when tap isn't an option. When the pipes break and pumps fail, of course, but also when you are, well, thirsty. "It's not so easy, walking down Third Avenue on a hot day, to get a glass of tap water," John D. Sicher Jr., editor and publisher of *Beverage Digest*, a trade publication, says. And, yes, all those PET bottles, which use about 40 percent less resin now than they did five years ago, really should be recycled, the bottlers all cry. ("Our vision is to no longer have our packaging viewed as waste but as a resource for future use," Scott Vitters, Coke's director of sustainable packaging, says.)

But please, don't insist that *we* rely on recycled content, is the bottlers' unspoken message, and let's collect the empties not through container deposit laws, which are funded by the beverage industry, but through beefed-up curbside or drop-off programs, which have, so far, been funded by taxpayers.

Finally, there's the "Americans deserve a choice" argument, offered by manufacturers whenever products with high social or environmental costs are challenged. It sounds patriotic, it promotes individualism, and it deflects responsibility from producers. If drinking bottled water, like smoking cigarettes and driving SUVs, is an individual choice, then manufacturers can't be blamed for any negative impacts, whether high cancer rates or oil wars.

Are environmental activists making too much of bottled water's externalities? Surely other redundant, status-oriented consumer products—the latest iteration of an iPod, for example—are worse for the environment, and for those affected by their manufacture (though granted, nobody buys an iPod a day). Michael Mascha, my water expert, is adamant on the topic: "All I want is to have a choice about what I drink. I want five or six waters to match a dining experience. Fine waters are a treat."

Mascha isn't drinking Dasani—a nonfine water—but he still has a dog in this fight, and he can't help marginalizing the opposition. "The backlash is the green movement," he says, "and it's antiglobalization. They say water shouldn't be a commodity, but why should water be free? Why is it different from food, which we also need to live, or shelter?"

The antiglobalization argument comes not from the mainstream environmental groups but from the pressure groups Food and Water Watch, which runs a "take back the tap" pledge campaign, and Corporate Accountability International. Antiglobalization groups have ideological roots in single-issue social and environmental campaigns (curbing sweatshop abuses and old-growth logging, for example). In recent years, such campaigns have converged to challenge the political power of large multinational corporations that, often by exercising free-trade agreements, are presumed to harm the environment and infringe upon human rights, local democracies, and cultural diversity.

Working to oppose what it calls "irresponsible and dangerous corporate actions around the world," CAI has targeted Nestlé, General Electric, and Philip Morris, among other companies. In the United States, its bottled-water campaign—

which taps both the environmental and the antiprivatization movements—has a multi-tiered agenda. First, it wants to demonstrate that most people can't discern between bottled and tap water. Second, it informs the public that most bottled water is "just tap" (which isn't, strictly speaking, true). Volunteers make their points about bottled water's carbon footprint, its sketchier regulation, and its expense compared to tap, and then they ask individuals, and local governments, to quit buying it. Depending on the city, CAI may also ask local officials to forswear selling public water to private bottlers.

The group also pushes for water bottlers in the United States to reveal their sources, to make public their breaches in quality (so far, no takers among bottlers, although California passed a law requiring bottlers to make such information available to consumers), and to quit threatening local control of water with their pumping and bottling. This last bit, against privatization of a public resource, is too outré for most mainstream news outlets to pick up on, perhaps because it raises sticky questions of ownership and control, and it offends many Americans' ideas about the primacy of capitalism. But while Corporate Accountability's mission to halt corporate control of the commons might be abstract to most bottled-water drinkers, it isn't the least bit abstract to Californians resisting Nestlé's efforts to build a plant in McCloud, near Mount Shasta, or to Floridians who swam in Crystal Springs until Nestlé began bottling it, or to those residents of Denmark and Fryeburg, Maine, still raging against Nestlé's boreholes and its big silver trucks.

The fate of Lovewell Pond might not interest the average person slapping down two bucks for a bottle of Poland Spring at a concession stand, but the issue of who controls water—Howard Dearborn's ultimate struggle—may in the long run be even more important than how many barrels of oil are burned to quench the nation's thirst. We can live without oil, but we can't live without water.

Chapter 8

TOWN MEETING

DELAYED TWO WEEKS by a storm that blankets western Maine with fifteen inches of heavy snow, Fryeburg's annual town meeting gets under way on the last day of March 2007. Of the seventy-eight articles on the warrant, the proposed water ordinance, number seventeen, is expected to draw the biggest fireworks. For more than a year, its substance and meaning have riven the town, pitted neighbors against neighbors, and focused an unholy amount of attention on the moral implications of cracking open a plastic bottle of water. Howard Dearborn is expected to finally unveil his study of Lovewell Pond, which he hopes will sway the town to vote against the ordinance. And Gene Bergoffen, after working for more than a year on that document, is hoping that Dearborn will fail.

It's a warm day, for Maine in March, and residents file into the truck bay of the fire station prepared for the long haul, with snacks, thermoses, and in Hannah Warren's case, knitting. Rows of folding chairs fill the fire station's truck bay, and town officers sit quietly at tables up front.

Since before Maine was carved from the territory of Massachusetts, the town meeting has been the state's most common
form of local government. All across New England, towns meet
in late winter or early spring to vote on operating budgets, laws,
and other matters for the community's operation over the following twelve months. Town meetings are social events, a welcome break from the long winter. They last all day, often broken
up by a potluck lunch. Bill McKibben writes in *Deep Economy:
The Wealth of Communities and the Durable Future*, "This may not
be the most efficient way to conduct the town's business—
electing a mayor and letting him decide might use fewer person-
hours in the course of a year. (Allowing a lobbyist to simply
write the legislation he's paid for is simplest of all.) But town
meeting is a school for educating residents about public affairs:
for making them citizens." Town meetings, says Frank Bryan, a
political scientist at the University of Vermont, are a place to
"practice face-to-face democracy as citizen legislators."

Peter Malia, the town attorney and a partner at the Hastings
Law Office (yes, those Hastings), moderates today's meeting.
He speaks quickly and without inflection, mindful of the thick
warrant he must wade through before he'll eat his supper. After
sprinting through the first four articles—which have to do
with the salaries of selectmen, selling town property, prepaying
taxes, and maintaining snowmobile trails—a motion is made to
take Article 17 next, out of order. "We need two thirds to pass
that," Malia says dispassionately. A voice vote approves the
switch, and Gene Bergoffen, the sponsor of the water ordinance, takes the mike.

"There have been a lot of personal attacks in this matter,

which have substantially confused people and undermined their trust in both people and this process," he says. In a room of winter-white people, Bergoffen looks tan and fit, with a close shave and a recent haircut. Bergoffen suggests the town delay voting on Article 17 until a day when "calm and impersonal focus," "objectivity," and "good science" can prevail.

Malia calls for a stand-up vote: by a margin of three bodies, the town of Fryeburg decides to debate the issue immediately.

The full text of Article 17 runs to eighteen pages, and it's been publicly available for only three weeks. But even if most people at the town meeting haven't actually read the thing, they know what it's fundamentally about: passing the water ordinance will allow Poland Spring to continue buying unlimited amounts of low-cost water from the Wards Brook aquifer while excluding other entities from pumping there. Within a newly drawn "wellhead protection zone," the ordinance will restrict what property owners can do on, or with, their land.

The ordinance seems to offer multiple layers of protection to the Wards Brook aquifer, from which the town drinks, but many townsfolk distrust it all the same. "Poland Spring thinks this is a huge aquifer," the Reverend Ken Turley had told me earlier, over tea in his kitchen. Turley is the pastor of the Church of the New Jerusalem, whose ladies would serve lunch on town-meeting day. "The company *will* need another bottling plant, and it will outspend anyone in order to do it. But once Poland Spring is in, you can't interfere with their profit. The town will end up buying water from Poland Spring. They're poised to take over the municipal system the minute it becomes profitable.

They're just waiting, like vultures. Ten years down the road, we'll be paying through the nose to get water."

Turley's concern about a takeover isn't idle: globalization activists fear that once citizens are accustomed to paying more for water—by buying it bottled instead of drinking it from the tap—they won't balk at paying higher rates to a private company, from outside the community, state, or even country, that runs their municipal system. Already the baseline is shifting. Across the country and around the world, private water companies have been making deals with public water utilities saddled with crumbling infrastructure and heavy debt. (Aware that *privatization* is considered by some a dirty word, some multinational water corporations—not to be confused with locally owned water companies—have switched to calling the arrangements "public-private partnerships," in which, broadly speaking, the municipality continues to own the utility, but the private firm operates and manages all or part of it.)

As documented in *Thirst: Fighting the Corporate Theft of Our Water*, these well-funded private companies offer to fix the pipes and deliver water, but many communities end up with higher rates, staff layoffs, less access to information, and declining service. When public utilities raise rates, the increase goes toward repairs, not Christmas bonuses for shareholders. Several U.S. cities have sued to regain control of their water systems from private companies. Other places—Gary, Indiana, and thirty communities in Boone County, West Virginia, among them—are happy with such arrangements.

"It's odd for a man in my position to say I don't trust Poland Spring," Turley continues, sipping his tea. "They argue as if it were a divine right to make as much money as they can. It would be cheaper for them to buy us off than to go through the court system." He turns to look out the window, into his snowy yard.

I ask what he wants Poland Spring to do. "Maybe profit sharing is the answer," Turley says, knowing it is too late for the company to pull out of town.

"Don't they already give money to the town?"

"Yes, but the donations are transparently manipulative."

"What would real generosity look like?"

Turley shrugs. "I don't know—it would just feel different. It's like the definition of pornography: I can't describe it but I know it when I see it. They could build up an endowment fund—they could show a concern for our economic ecosystem."

When Jim Wilfong talks about taxing Poland Spring's water withdrawals in Maine, he sometimes drops in the word *Alaska*. It's a loaded reference, likely to spark thoughts of the Alaska Permanent Fund, a state-run program that puts an annual dividend from the sale of North Slope oil in the pocket of nearly every Alaska resident (in 2007, the dividend was $1,654). The reference links oil with water, and it reminds folks that the state's natural resources are just that: naturally occurring. (Though here the similarities stop: bottled water costs more than gasoline, on a per liter basis, despite the fact that oil is far more expensive to pull from the ground, to process, and to transport.)

As residents approach the mike in the fire station to speak about the water ordinance, it becomes clear that while some distrust those who wrote the document or have a moral objection to selling water for profit, many others are concerned mostly with economic justice, with the whopping disparity between what Nestlé pays for water (nothing, in those towns where it owns or leases land) and what it makes by selling it. "People have been talking about balance," says Ken Brown, a burly man in a plaid jacket. "We have a gentleman here that's trying to run a farm, and he has to jump through hoops [if the ordinance passes] and spend money if he breaks a level of ten thousand gallons a day. And he's up against a company that has stacks and stacks of water at our town meeting that is worth billions of dollars." Brown turns and points toward the firehouse wall, where cases of Poland Spring water are stacked. Heads turn and nod.

It is easy to play the farm card in Fryeburg: agriculture is a mainstay of the local economy. There's the beans, corn, and sod, and there's all the agritourists too: two hundred thousand of them a year drawn to the state's largest agricultural fair. No one wants to hurt a farmer, Brown knows. "We give Nestlé the benefit of six hundred thousand gallons a day for their profit," he continues, "while we make this guy over here . . . go before the planning board to get their okay. I'm sorry—somewhere along the line, I don't know where the balance is." He turns his palms up and pantomimes a scale.

Personal use is a concern too: will town residents have enough good water as its population grows, as the climate warms, and droughts, like the one that hit in 2005, become more frequent? There is talk of reopening a rail line between Portland and Fryeburg: will it bring more businesses or manu-facturing plants that require water? And what about the Saco

River, that mythic pathway to the mountains but also, let's face it, a mighty engine of tourism dollars? If pumping affects the aquifer, someday it will affect the river too.

Not every ordinance skeptic, of course, has high-minded concerns about algal blooms or the survival of family farms and other independent businesses. Some people just want rate relief. (The town's water bills are about average: in 2006 Fryeburg had the 95th highest rate out of 157 water utilities in the state.) "If we're gonna sell our water, let's make some money on it," another speaker says. In 2006, Poland Spring sold $843 million worth of Maine water.

"Hear, hear," voices mutter.

I had recently called Bill Black, the state's deputy public advocate, to ask about the town's water rates. According to his back-of-the-envelope calculations, if Poland Spring bought out Pure Mountain Springs, then the Fryeburg Water Company could sell directly to Poland Spring, with no middleman. "If they bought from the utility at the same rate they paid Pure Mountain, at the volume they pumped in 2004," Black had said, "the need for revenue paid by other customers would drop close to zero." He paused. "People might actually be *paid*." It was starting to sound like Alaska.

After a half hour of impressively civil discourse, it's Howard Dearborn's turn. In a white tennis sweater, his hands empty and his voice shaky, he says, "My name is Howard Dearborn. I live on Lovewell Pond. I've been a resident of Fryeburg for more than fifty years. What else do you want to know?" He scans the room with the same expectant look he wore when telling Miles

Waite his pump was sucking air. Dearborn continues, "I've been insulted and called a liar." He pauses. "The information in *Water Waves*, my newsletter, is correct. I have spent thirty-three thousand dollars on a survey of Lovewell Pond. I'm trying to save Lovewell Pond and also Fryeburg." He returns to his seat, done. If there's a smoking gun in the Waite report, Dearborn is keeping it holstered.

A woman with short silver hair and painted fingernails steps up. "This is a trillion-dollar corporation in a three-thousand-population town," she says. The audience suddenly perks up. Speaking as if the CEO of Nestlé Waters were standing in front of her, eyes downcast after cracking a baseball through her window, Emily Fletcher fires away. "You may win in a court of law, but the burden of proof in small-town America is to win the public's trust. And I'm not trusting because I don't know what the fine print means or says." Last October, she says, the planning board approved the tanker station in East Fryeburg; it favored Poland Spring over a group of neighbors, forcing them into court, and costing them tens of thousands of dollars. She lets that sink in, then continues in a tone of controlled scolding.

"We have one vote: we want to know if this ordinance is in our best interest. It feels to me like the public needs an attorney to represent *them*, what *they* want." Now the town's residents—lots of them—begin to clap. Fletcher is expressing *their* frustration, *their* sense of disenfranchisement. Heads crane for a better look. Fletcher has standing in this town. She's the town librarian, the daughter of the previous generation's town doctor, and like Tom Brennan an alumnus of Maine's Bates College. "I want to know that the taxpaying public, their lands, their interests, their opportunities, now and in the future, are respected," Fletcher says. "I want to know that they come first, and that all these trucks hauling in and out of here, every day, come second." Again, applause.

Fletcher sits down, looking a bit overwhelmed, and the town votes.

It's been said by water activists that the fight over water is a fight for democracy itself. And of course there's nothing like the arrival of a large corporation in a small town to test the limits of civility, self-interest, and free speech. People who've never read their town bylaws or land-use tables get out their dictionaries, neighbors come out against neighbors, the feet of elected or appointed officials are held to the fire. The pattern has been the same in states all over the country. Nestlé arrives, property is purchased, information is presented at endless meetings, and a juggernaut is set in motion. Inevitably, some residents feel excluded from the process: they feel that documents aren't made available in a timely manner, that questions aren't fully answered. Planning boards move to closed session. Rumors of corruption fly; citizens sue to halt operations, injunctions are filed, then appealed. It is wearing, and it is expensive.

In Maine and elsewhere, bottling opponents have accused Nestlé of placing "operatives" in town ahead of their arrival—to grease the wheels, scope the competition, and make sure key local officials are onboard. Whether or not it's true, some believe Gene Bergoffen plays that role in Fryeburg. He moved to town five years before the town started fighting over water (though he summered here as a child). A former Washington attorney, he quickly tried to work himself into the local fabric, becoming a trustee of a regional conservation group, seeking a position on the board of directors at a nearby hospital, becoming the head of the Lovewell Pond Association, a member of the town's planning board, and finally its chairman. Dearborn alleges that Bergoffen is "getting paid by Nestlé to screw things up."

Bergoffen denies the claim, of course, and says he currently has no connection to Nestlé, though he was, from 1989 to 1997, the CEO of the National Private Truck Council, which lobbies on behalf of private trucking fleets and counts among its thousand-plus members Nestlé Waters North America. Bergoffen is currently president of MaineWay Services, which consults with trucking fleets and other clients (not Nestlé) on issues of trucking safety, management, and trucking policy.

It's easy to cast water battles as David-and-Goliath dramas, with small-town innocents up against rich and experienced corporations. Peter Crabb, who lives downstream of Nestlé's New Tripoli, Pennsylvania, operation, summarized his experience with the company in a post to AlterNet: "This Swiss corporation came into our tiny rural American community and bullied residents and bribed local officials to look the other way while they had their way with our water supply." Now diesel trucks clog the narrow roadways, he says, and lower water levels in the creek have decimated fish populations. In Mecosta County, Michigan, where Nestlé bottles springwater under the Ice Mountain label, the company promised good jobs at the bottling plant, but they didn't materialize. Instead, say anti-Nestlé activists, the company hired temporary workers, who receive no benefits and no compensation when they are laid off.

Residents of McCloud, California, population eighteen hundred, learned in the fall of 2003 of Nestlé's intentions to pump and bottle, under the Arrowhead label, 522 million gallons of springwater a year. Its plant, at a million square feet, would be the largest in the nation. The water flows from two glaciers on Mount Shasta and feeds some of the world's best trout-fishing streams. To some, the promise of sixty jobs looked like a good deal: the local lumber mill had recently shut down, students were migrating from the local high school to one in Mount Shasta, and the town needed a new fire truck. But other residents thought Nestlé was ripping them off.

The company proposed to pay McCloud three hundred thousand dollars a year—about a tenth of a cent per gallon of water—going up to four hundred thousand dollars in year ten of a hundred-year contract. The fees were well under market rates, and the company would have the right to drill unlimited boreholes and pump unlimited groundwater. When the McCloud Watershed Council polled local citizens, it found 77 percent opposed to the contract. The council also considered the environmental reviews grossly inadequate and found that truck traffic would be disruptive and dangerous. To those residents of Fryeburg keeping tabs from three thousand miles away, the scenario sounded distressingly familiar.

Is Nestlé really subverting democracy, as the antiprivatization groups suggest? The company participates in informational meetings, it shares its data (though perhaps not all of it), it pays for endless studies of aquifers, trucking routes, and traffic. Votes are taken. By and large, citizens rise to the occasion: they share information, collect their own data, and participate at a level that is, for many, unprecedented. This is democracy in action.

But only to a point. When a large corporation—with all the lawyers, PR professionals, and hydrological reports that money can buy—goes up against individual citizens, it's hardly a level playing field. It's nothing for Nestlé to make six-figure donations—perfectly legal—so that towns with perennial budget shortfalls can repair their roads or buildings. Money talks, especially in communities with high unemployment and a low tax base. Large corporations, because they make campaign contributions, employ hundreds, and add to state revenue, have friends in high places. Their permits are rubber stamped and they receive exemptions from statutes and grandfather status for activities no longer permitted.

In the spring of 2007, while Nestlé shareholders gathered in Switzerland for their annual meeting, the Sierra Club, a Nestlé shareholder, led a gathering of concerned citizens at the company's Greenwich, Connecticut, headquarters. There, Ruth Caplan, chair of the Sierra Club's Water Privatization Task Force, said that Nestlé has consistently failed to obtain explicit consent from communities affected by bottling operations at nearby water sources that serve the communities' water needs. Her group called on Nestlé to "respect the right of local communities to exercise democratic control over the use of their water," to let town residents vote on Nestlé activities, and to quit using its disproportionate resources to influence their decisions.

Activists repeatedly link small-town struggles against Nestlé in the United States with grassroots battles against transnationals in the developing world. Portrayed as good (poor people without water) against evil (corporations that buy and sell water), those struggles seem clear-cut to me. But the situation in Fryeburg isn't so black-and-white. A faction here is okay with Poland Spring if it means the company will build a plant, which will bring jobs and money into town, or even if it simply agrees to make steady payments to the town. One could argue that pumping water in western Maine denies no one access to water, nor does the company force people to buy its green-wrapped bottles. Maybe not now, counter the activists, but that day may come: drought may strike this region—or a region elsewhere—and citizens may find private water trucks running when their taps do not. Remember, water is essential for life, and communities that don't have it will either find a way to buy more or they will disappear. When that day arrives, whose hand do you want on the tap?

After two hours of debate in Fryeburg's fire station, the water ordinance is defeated by a vote of 125 to 53. David of Maine has beaten the giant from Switzerland. But the reaction is subdued— the crowd looks a little stunned. Peter Malia quickly reads the warrant's next article, and the town meeting grinds on.

I sense relief among the Nestlé opponents, but no one is celebrating quite yet. The ordinance may have been one referendum on Nestlé, but the company still has many other ways to sink its roots into the town of Fryeburg—among them, legal challenges and new proposals. As the town manager ruefully says to me afterward, "The saga continues."

In mid-April of 2007, less than two weeks after Fryeburg's town meeting, attorney Scott Anderson, representing the citizens group Western Maine Residents for Rural Living, and attorney Catherine R. Connors, representing Nestlé Waters North America, stand before the seven robed justices of Maine's Supreme Judicial Court, in Portland. At long last, Anderson will argue that the tanker station in East Fryeburg isn't an "allowed use" in a rural residential zone. He'll also be arguing, on behalf of a Denmark landowner, against that town's decision to allow Nestlé to pump springwater, on the grounds that it doesn't meet the environmental and commercial standards for bulk-water extraction. Connors is here to defend both the pumping and the trucking.

Hannah Warren, Emily Fletcher, and Scott Gamwell, a certified public accountant who lives in East Fryeburg near the proposed tanker station, drove down from Fryeburg this morning to watch the proceedings. They take seats at one end of the stately, columned room and watch with dismay, but not surprise, as Gene Bergoffen sweeps in and takes a seat at the opposite end of the room, with two public-relations executives from Nestlé. And then the arguments begin. For someone unaccustomed to the frank language of business, the next fifty-four minutes are a revelation.

The Denmark case hinges on a clause in Maine's bulk-water transport law, enacted in 1987, that says tankers of water can move over municipal boundaries for commercial purposes only if (1) its transport won't constitute a threat to public health, safety, or welfare; (2) the water isn't available naturally in the location to which it will be transported; and (3) failure to authorize transport of the water would create a substantial hardship to the potential recipient of the water.

The first and second clauses aren't a big deal for Nestlé, or

Anderson. The third clause, however, is huge. What does "substantial hardship" actually mean?

"Economic hardship," Connors says, starting things off.

Chief Justice Leigh Ingalls Saufley asks for a clarification. "You'll lose an opportunity to make *greater* profits?"

Well, yes, Connors says. "Not only will we be unable to meet projected demand but also existing. As the population increases in towns with facilities, less water is available for Poland Spring."

"Doesn't that show it's a finite resource?" Saufley asks. "If you arrived at a point where you have to go to Denmark and pump out multiple gallons . . ." She trails off. "Why should we accept an argument that a loss of market share is enough to show substantial hardship that allows your client to continue to truck water out of the state?"

Gripping a wooden lectern, worn at the top from years of such gripping, Connors explains that Poland Spring's pumping is sustainable, that the aquifer recharges. "If Denmark increases its needs, we'll go elsewhere." Her voice quavers, just a little.

"Isn't it an upside-down pyramid," asks Saufley, "as you extract more water and take it away, local towns lose their water capacity and you move elsewhere, and you create more desire for bottled water elsewhere, which means that this finite natural resource in Maine begins to be the source for a greater and greater demand, nationally? If your incapacity to [meet] market share gets you substantial hardship, it is endless."

"It's rechargeable," Connors replies.

After a short break the court turns to the matter of the East Fryeburg trucking station—not its pros or cons, but whether the case is ripe for this court to contemplate—and then the justices adjourn. Their decision isn't expected for several months. On the question of bulk-water extraction, it doesn't look good for Poland Spring. Only two justices questioned the attorneys, but they both seemed sympathetic to Western Maine Residents for Rural Living and skeptical that Nestlé Waters needed Denmark's water.

While Gamwell, Warren, and Fletcher, among others, await the court's decision, Jim Wilfong is busy working another angle. Years ago, his group, H2O for ME, had attempted, but failed, to pass a first-in-the-nation bottled-water tax. When Wilfong vows to launch a second referendum, Nestlé—perhaps feeling uneasy about which way the substantial-hardship case will go—agrees to a compromise. The company, along with Wilfong, state appointees, and other stakeholders, hammers out legislation in the state capital that requires commercial extractors to submit to stricter environmental reviews, which consider impacts on entire watersheds, a more thorough and public reviewing process of their permit applications, and subsequent groundwater monitoring paid for by companies. The deal is done well before the Supreme Judicial Court announces its decision.

"This is a real victory for democracy," Wilfong tells me on the phone, just after the bill is signed. "It takes a big chunk out of absolute dominion." No longer can landowners pump all the groundwater they please.

Nestlé underplays the legislation. "It's not an appreciable change for us," Tom Brennan says, because Nestlé already considers all the environmental impacts. (At new bottling plants, sure, Wilfong says, but Nestlé doesn't do that for individual extraction wells.)

Wilfong believes the legislation helps clarify ownership of groundwater: "That is the big issue. Not just in Maine but around the country and around the world. As clean water grows scarce, who is going to own it, and who is going to control it? And isn't it insane policy to let multinationals control something so important?"

The story of Nestlé in Fryeburg, then, isn't just about Howard Dearborn's pond, or the truck traffic from the proposed tanker station near Scott Gamwell's house. It's not just about whether a company is creating good Maine jobs. The story of Nestlé in Fryeburg is, in its own weird way, the story of globalization, and what this town learns about water's ownership and control will matter to all of us as water scarcity—"the most underappreciated global environmental challenge of our time," according to the Worldwatch Institute—begins to hit home.

Three months after Scott Anderson and Catherine Connors presented their oral arguments in Portland, the court issues its opinion. It remands the Fryeburg case, regarding the trucking station, back to that town's planning board and orders it to consider other criteria in the town's comprehensive plan. In the matter of Denmark, the court decides that Poland Spring will indeed suffer substantial hardship if it can't get enough water to feed its bottling plants. The permit stands.

Anderson, who thought he had a decent shot, is crushed. (And the Reverend Ken Turley suddenly looks like a prophet for saying, months earlier, "They argue as if it were a divine right to make as much money as they can.") "The substantial-hardship test addressed ownership and control," Anderson says, "and now those issues don't figure into it." The court, in other words, punted. Now, if companies can show that not taking water will hurt their bottom line—and Nestlé can show this in every Maine town it approaches—the water is theirs for the taking.

In a philosophical mode, Anderson says, "The state legislature looks at jobs and economic benefits: I understand and appreciate that. The legislature sees this as a local issue. They'll let it go on until it grows and becomes a problem. And it will, as the population grows. We see it already in the West, and it's going to happen here too."

In early autumn, Fryeburg is still simmering. Nestlé closes on the Bailey's property, roughly forty acres over the Wards Brook aquifer, and digs up buried fuel tanks. Does the company plan to build a bottling plant here? It won't say for sure. The WE Corporation, formed by Jeff Walker and Rick Eastman to pump from their well off Porter Road, has failed to find a water buyer and has offered to sell its land and well to the town. Control of the watershed seems to be shifting.

With the Denmark decision behind them, Dearborn and his cohort are now focusing their energy on the planning board, which will soon be reconsidering the tanker station permit. Is it, in fact, a low-impact business, compatible with other allowed uses in a rural residential district? The Poland Spring trucks on Portland Street are already so loud, say townsfolk, that you can't talk in your living room with the windows open. "These are huge issues for a little town to deal with," says Mike Dana, a filmmaker who moved here from New York to get away from truck traffic. "If you can put this in a rural residential district, it sets a precedent. You can put them all over Fryeburg, eighty percent of which is zoned rural residential."

This time around, the water activists are hoping to keep Gene Bergoffen from voting. "He consults with the trucking industry," Scott Gamwell says. "That's a conflict of interest." Nestlé's lawyers disagree: "Not only is such knowledge not a basis for disqualification," they write to the town's attorney, "but should be welcomed." Meanwhile, as a sort of insurance policy, 150 Fryeburg residents sign a petition calling for a moratorium on permits for "omitted uses" in rural residential zones—essentially, a halt to places where tanker trucks can fill up with water.

It turns out they don't need it. When the planning board meets in early October, watched by three Nestlé representatives, plus a Nestlé stenographer, the board votes, three to one, to keep Bergoffen from voting on the trucking station. The chairman collects his papers, strides out, and within half an hour resigns his position. Following an emotional town meeting in November—at which the tanker site is compared to a missile-launch facility and Hugh Hastings threatens the town with higher water rates should Poland Spring pull out of town—three of the remaining four board members vote no on the tanker station.

The Nestlé opponents are pleased with their wins (passing the moratorium, then ousting Bergoffen, which led to the defeat of the tanker-station permit), but they know too much now to imagine Poland Spring will disappear. The company owns or leases quite a bit of land in the area, Fryeburg has copious good water, and the market for Poland Spring is only growing.

It's hard to imagine Lovewell Pond or the Wards Brook aquifer drying up, like the Aral Sea when large-scale irrigation of the desert got under way, but that's probably what they thought in Kazakhstan fifty years ago too. (And in Atlanta as recently as a year ago.) Aquifers that feed streams and lakes are invisible, and humans are generally oblivious to incremental changes in their environment—that's why miners used to employ canaries. Crises, though, generally get our attention. The crack-up of the *Exxon Valdez* begot double-hulled tankers, the conflagration of the Cuyahoga River inspired the Clean Water Act, and the putrid state of the Mississippi in New Orleans spurred the Safe Drinking Water Act.

I visit the canary of Lovewell Pond. Dearborn looks thinner and paler than he did several months ago, but he's as feisty as ever. I ask him about the buffer zone around the town's wells, and before I know it the conversation devolves into a debate over the nation's antipollution laws. I think they should be strengthened, but Dearborn, who ran a manufacturing plant for fifty years, interprets my position as antibusiness. He shouts at me, so I move on to what should be a neutral topic.

"How's the lake level now?"

"The level between the lake and the river is almost zero," he says sourly.

"How do you know that?" I'm impressed with his precision but want to know how he comes to it.

"I know within an inch," he says, his voice rising again.

"Okay, but how?"

"I know because I marked Moose Rock out there, using known elevations and working with a transit—do you know what a transit is?" Dearborn speaks in an accusing tone, one he's never used with me before. I nod, picturing the surveying instrument. "I've been watching that rock for fifty years. And when it's almost at zero, that means water is no longer moving out of the pond into the Saco or into the pond from the Saco." He pauses and stares at me, hard. "You think I made this up? I'm no dummy." I nod again, blinking away sudden tears. "You don't care about the lake, do you? You haven't even seen it."

"I have seen it," I sputter. Has Dearborn forgotten my previous visits, my excursion in his own boat? "I'd like to see the rock again."

"I'll show you," he growls at me, "but I might push you in."

This remark doesn't break the tension because Dearborn is serious. He smiles grimly; he's angry with me now. He thinks I don't believe him, or that I question his judgment. Mike Dana, who's been listening to this escalation with dismay, suddenly stands up.

"I'll take you out," he says.

We stand on the sandy beach and Dana points at the painted rock, just down the shore. "I'm sorry," he says. "I don't know why he gets this way—he's just so passionate about the issue."

"No, I'm sorry," I say, grateful that my back is to the house and Dearborn can't see me wipe my eyes. "I didn't mean to make him angry."

"It's not you—it's everyone." Apparently, Dearborn has been snapping at anyone who doesn't immediately sympathize with his cause, at anyone who questions his authority. His Lear-like ravings shake me, but they underscore the intensity of Dearborn's situation. He's fighting a giant, and he feels he's running out of options and time. Again, Dana points to the rock. "I have to keep pointing because I know he's looking at me."

The lake is low—it is always low in the fall—and we walk onto Dearborn's dock, which casts a shadow on a lake bottom blanketed in brown algae. "It used to be sandy and clear here," Dana says. "Howard used to have waterskiing parties." The ski boat is tied on the right, and the smaller skiff, the one Dearborn built, bobs on the left. If Wards Brook were flushing the pond, Dearborn and Dana believe, the algae wouldn't be here. The Waite report concluded that the pond's phosphorus levels were high enough to spur the growth of aquatic weeds, and that reducing spring flow into the pond, through excessive pumping, would not only reduce the already low flushing rate but also allow the Saco River to become a more dominant factor in its water quality. Given the excessive phosphorus levels in the Saco, Waite said, "This change could have a detrimental effect on the pond."

When I go inside to fetch my bag, Dearborn barks, "Come on, I want to show you something." He walks stiffly to his old Buick station wagon and we drive the short distance to Dearborn Precision Tubular Products. There seem to be fewer tanker trucks in town lately, Dearborn says en route. "I think they've hurt the aqua-fire." Maybe. It's hard to say what's going on underground; Poland Spring checks its Fryeburg wells and gauges monthly but gives data to the town hall annually.

Inside, Dearborn breezes past the receptionist—"Good morning, Howard"—and through the cubicles to the hangar-like work area. "Morning, Mr. Dearborn," a dozen men in work clothes call out. We tour through the computerized milling, drilling, and boring machines. "We specialize in long parts with holes through them," Dearborn says. He runs his gnarled hands over tubes smooth as water, inside and out, many of them machined to hold instruments and sensors for use in oil-drilling rigs and nuclear power plants.

Why did Dearborn, so angry with me fifteen minutes ago, bring me here? Obviously, he wants credibility. He'd built this place, with its two hundred employees, from the ground up; he'd invented many of these machines and processes. Therefore, when Howard Dearborn says the lake is damaged, that his pump is sucking air, and that the plant growth is unusual, it must be true.

But still, I wonder, why? Why spend five years and one hundred thousand dollars fighting Nestlé? Dearborn could be enjoying a glorious retirement, tinkering in his shop and puttering in his boat, his airplane, and his snowmobile. "I'm stubborn," he says. "I started it and I want to finish it." But Nestlé, I worry, might finish Dearborn. He isn't in great health, and it doesn't seem that too many young folks are ready to take his place. Who would write and mail the newsletters, pay the lawyers, and hire the independent scientists? His son, who lives in Ohio, doesn't want his house, and there are no grandkids to swim in his pond, even if it were weed-free.

As I drive out of town, I remember what Dearborn had told me about his arrival in Fryeburg, fifty years ago. "I couldn't get a septic system because the code-enforcement officer wouldn't come out," he'd said. "I couldn't buy hardware in town, I had to contract out for electrical work from Portland." Why? "Because I'm an *outsider*, a flatlander," he shouted. "I had to drill my own well. It cost me ten thousand dollars to get water."

I think about that well, and I realize it wasn't that long ago that Hugh Hastings, the consummate Fryeburg insider, had stood on Dearborn's deck and pointed out the land he owned, and Dearborn had granted him access to property on which he would drill another well. Then Hastings had turned around and sold that water to Pure Mountain Springs, which sold it in turn to Nestlé. What had seemed such a simple gesture, providing a path through the woods, turned out to be the beginning of the end.

Chapter 9

SOMETHING TO DRINK?

MORE THAN A year after my first visit to Lovewell Pond, a part of Fryeburg is still struggling against Nestlé. And the company, like a rebuffed lover in denial of reality—or like Jake Gittes, the detective in *Chinatown*—won't let go. Poland Spring opens a small office in downtown Fryeburg and in early December runs ads inviting locals to stop in for coffee and "straight talk" with Mark Dubois, who has inherited the infamous Fryeburg situation from Tom Brennan. (Brennan has been promoted to senior natural resources manager, and his purview now extends from the Northeast through the mid-Atlantic down to the Southern states.) Finding business slow, Dubois offers free cases of water to the first fifty visitors who can answer a trivia question correctly (who said, "Ask not what your country can do for you"?).

Infuriated, Howard Dearborn organizes a Boston Tea Party, offering ten dollars to the first fifty who show up at his place to dump their Poland Spring bottles into Lovewell Pond. The Saturday-afternoon event draws about forty-five people including two crashers from Nestlé who try to distribute information countering Dearborn's claims. A few townsfolk sternly tell them, "You're not welcome here," but they don't quit the property until Dearborn gets in their face, shaking one of them by the shoulders. "This is *my* pour," he says in a steely tone. "Hold your *own* pour on your *own* land."

The following Monday, Nestlé appeals the planning board's decision on the tanker station. Fryeburg's board of appeals rejects the challenge, and the case moves, once again, to the courts. "It's not over," Mark Dubois says. Regarding the end of the pipeline from the Denmark spring, he adds, "There are four points to a compass." Translation: Nestlé will find a way to get that water into trucks, perhaps from another property at the pipe's end.

The New Year brings startling news: Nestlé, after months of secret negotiations, has purchased Pure Mountain Springs—its assets and its land. While Tom Brennan hopes eliminating the middleman will "get a rational dialog going" in Fryeburg, some fear the deal will only consolidate Nestlé's control of the Wards Brook aquifer, a key step on its way to building a local bottling plant. "They're working every angle," Jim Wilfong says. "In a few years they'll control all the springs: that's the end game."

For now, the only constants in this town are the gleaming tanker trucks sloshing with Wards Brook water. Howard Dearborn, postpour, starts work on his next *Water Waves* newsletter, now with Mike Dana at his side. Since quitting the planning board, Gene Bergoffen rarely shows up at town meetings. Hannah Warren, though still committed to the cause, is now preoccupied with her newly opened bakery. Jim Wilfong, after helping to pass tighter state water-extraction legislation, has expanded his activism to the federal level. Emily Fletcher, who pleaded so emotionally for local control at town meetings, continues to speak out, and to cringe whenever someone mentions they've seen her declarations on YouTube.

Meanwhile, across the nation and around the globe, rising temperatures, population growth, drought, and increased pollution and development continue to strain water resources—its distribution, availability, and quality. The coming scarcity will hurt the growth of jobs, housing, and businesses. Water experts predict shortages will pit communities and states against each other, states' rights against national interests, the rich against the poor, cities against villages, corporations against individuals, and humans against other creatures that compete with us for water— such as delta smelt in the Sacramento–San Joaquin River delta, or mussels and sturgeon in Georgia, where water allocations that favor endangered species have angered upstream consumers. Scarcity will force us to change our minds—and, it is to be hoped, our behavior—about everything from landscaping to how often we eat meat.

Already, larger bodies of water across the United States are changing in ways that worry scientists. Lakes Superior, Huron, and Michigan, which contain nearly 20 percent of the world's fresh surface water, have been in steep decline since the late 1990s, with water levels lower than normal because of reduced snowmelt and increased evaporation; the lakes are also warmer because of higher ambient temperatures. (Nestlé pumps 114 billion gallons a year from groundwater that feeds Lake Michigan, and Coke and Pepsi recently signed contracts with Detroit to bottle and ship Great Lakes water.)

In Lake Tahoe, increased sediment and pollution—a result of development—fuel the growth of algae, which absorb light and increase the water's temperature. In the 1960s, a Secchi disk—the same black-and-white circle Miles Waite threw overboard on Lovewell Pond—was visible to one hundred and two feet; in 2006, the lake's visibility was reduced to sixty-seven feet. In the Southeast, the worst drought in a hundred years has lowered reservoir levels in Alabama to the point where pumps, sucking mud, have shut down. Before the Army Corps of Engineers slashed water releases for endangered species, Atlanta, toward the end of 2007, had enough readily available drinking water to last just a few months, and Georgia is feuding with Alabama and Florida over allocations. Workers at one dried-up Southeastern reservoir now *mow* it. With its creek and spring gone dry, the tiny town of Orme, Tennessee, imports water in a truck. Residents race home to wash clothes, cook meals, and take showers during the three daily hours the spigot runs.

Global warming will affect the quality of our water as well as its quantity. In warmer temperatures, more microbes flourish in surface water; if they move into pipes, they could feed biofilms, which include pathogens, in the distribution system. Climatologists agree that global warming will make the earth, on average, wetter. But more rain and snow will fall closer to the poles, and precipitation will fall during sporadic, intense storms, rather than smaller, more frequent ones. A warmer climate will bring more frequent floods, which will increase the flow of sediment and polluted runoff into our water supplies. Floods will damage pipes that move good water in and bad water out. In drier areas, perversely, we'll see more droughts.

Not only will there be less water for home consumption, industry, and agriculture, there will be less water to dilute pollutants.

A report released by the Union of Concerned Scientists in July of 2007 predicted, in a worst-case scenario, that the White Mountain region of New England, which includes the headwaters of the Saco River, could experience sixty-six days a year with temperatures over ninety degrees, compared to ten days now. With less snowpack to feed streams and aquifers, plus more movement of moisture from earth to the atmosphere on hot days, rivers will dry up.

Making matters worse, the warmer the weather, the more water we all use. Richard Lamming of the British Soft Drinks Association quantified the uptick: "For every degree the temperature rises above fourteen C [57.2 Fahrenheit], sales of water increase by 5.2 percent. This means that at twenty-eight C [82.4 Fahrenheit] sales of water double."

Our government might be able to do something about the weather; it certainly has the power to protect watersheds and help cities and towns maintain infrastructure. Unfortunately, that isn't happening. The Bush administration has scaled back enforcement of the Clean Water Act, which keeps waterways fishable and swimmable. It has failed to adequately fund basic maintenance projects, such as repairing or upgrading hundred-year-old water mains. The EPA, on Bush's watch, declined to set and enforce limits for dozens of industrial contaminants. In 1995, Congress let the Superfund tax lapse, leaving the EPA struggling to address cleanup needs today. In 2006, Bush rolled back the Toxics Release Inventory: now industries report less frequently on the contaminants they release to the environment.

Without substantial change, the forecast for tap water looks bad. And the forecast for bottled water, as pristine sources grow scarce and private companies gain control of those that remain, looks good.

Renting a house in rural Dutchess County, New York, I glimpse the future when our taps, one night, yield nothing. We'd come home late and headed upstairs to brush our teeth, but the pump, apparently, wasn't working. One five-hour plumber visit later, and we learn it's not the electrical system, it's the well: gone dry. Suddenly, all my water research is eerily relevant. The plumber returns and together we try, unsuccessfully, to drop a line 460 feet into the well to see if we can hit water. "Don't you have a transducer?" I ask, thinking of Rich Fortin's magic bob.

Next comes a pump test—performed by a guy with a hose, a scrap of paper, and a pencil stub—which reveals a recharge rate of just 7.8 gallons an hour. (A half-inch garden hose, under normal water pressure, can go through more than five hundred gallons an hour.) Where did all the water go? Hard to say. We repair a leaky toilet, then we learn a springwater company is operating a few miles away. Of course I wonder if it's affecting our water supply, but there's no way to know: the county has done limited groundwater mapping, every well on our road is a different depth, some wells have already been moved or drilled deeper. It looks as if our landlord will have to do this too. I buy two gallons of locally sourced springwater, suffer some minor tummy trouble, and take sponge baths using water collected by the basement dehumidifier. It's fun for a while—a little like camping. But the novelty doesn't last. In another week the rental is over, and the problem becomes someone else's.

In another few weeks, my water issue is quality, not quantity. We visit friends in rural Long Island. No one in the house, a summer rental, drinks from the tap: some don't like the taste of the well water, some are scared of contamination from the gasoline additive MTBE, a persistent problem in Long Island aquifers, and from surrounding grape and sod farms, which use a lot of fertilizer and herbicides. Corporate Accountability International claims that misleading marketing of bottled water as the only place to get a safe drink has undermined the public's confidence in tap. In this instance, however, knowledge of our environment has worked this trick all on its own: in the pantry are a 2.5-gallon jug of Deer Park, a 2.5-gallon jug of Poland Spring, a liter of Perrier, and a couple of bottles of San Pellegrino—all Nestlé products. Feeling haunted by that company, I ask my friends if they own shares in it. No, they shrug—it's merely coincidence.

Within a few days all those containers are empty. The tap doesn't scare me, not over the short haul, but I'm not convinced the children should drink it. In a quandary, and resentful about placing our health in the hands of a company with a clouded corporate history—Nestlé has marketed baby formula to African mothers, which has led them to give up breast-feeding; used underage and coerced labor on cocoa farms in Ivory Coast; and stymies citizens across the United States who are trying to decide their communities' fate—I fire up my carbon-spewing car and drive to the store to buy water, the cheapest non-Nestlé brand on the shelf.

Protecting drinking water isn't just a matter of money: it takes political will to allocate and spend it. But the more people who, like me on Long Island, opt out of drinking tap water, the less political support there may be for taking care of public water supplies—for protecting upstream watersheds, wrangling with polluters, tightening water-quality standards, and replacing old pipes. Distanced from public systems, committed bottled-water drinkers will have little incentive to support bond issues and other methods, including rate increases, of upgrading municipal water treatment. (Nestlé commissioned a poll of bottled-water drinkers and found 72 percent favored spending tax money to improve water infrastructure, but the poll didn't ask respondents if they'd support *raising* taxes or water rates to do so.) It's a self-fulfilling prophecy: the fewer who drink from public supplies, the worse the water will get, and the more bottled water we'll need.

It's happening already in India, where fewer and fewer city dwellers drink from the tap. Without financial support from ratepayers, public utilities are having a tough time delivering water to anyone. That isn't a problem for the rich: they can afford to find water elsewhere. But poor people in the developing world, usually women and girls, end up waiting in line for hours to buy buckets of water that cost far more than the stuff they could have gotten from the tap, if the utility were doing its job. In Lagos, Nigeria, the poor pay four to ten times more for a liter of water than do people hooked up to water mains; in Lima, they pay seventeen times more; in Karachi, twenty-eight to eighty-three times more; in Jakarta, up to sixty times more; and in Port-au-Prince, Haiti, up to one hundred times more.

Is a two-tiered system—bottled for the rich, bilge for the poor—that far-fetched? Will the future look like something out of the Broadway musical *Urinetown*, where only those with money can afford to drink water (and eliminate)? Sadly, no. Water utilities are well aware that residents drink or cook with only 1 to 2 percent of the water that enters their home: most water goes for lawn watering, car washing, toilet flushing, showers, and laundry. Why spend millions to bring water up to high standards, goes one line of thinking, if so little is actually consumed?

"If we didn't have to spend billions (and soon to be trillions) of dollars on pipes, treatment plants, and chemicals, could we better spend that money on other needs?" Breck Speed, chairman of the Mountain Valley Spring Company in Hot Springs, Arkansas, wrote in an editorial. "Does it make sense—indeed, is it even possible—for local governments to attempt to bring tap water up to the higher quality of bottled water?" Taking an exploratory step in this direction, the EPA in December of 2006 held a listening session on whether safe-drinking-water rules could be met, in limited situations, by using bottled water instead of tap.

Until recently, the town of Westford, Massachusetts (population 20,754, including my father), drank unfiltered and unchlorinated water pumped from wells near the sinuous and verdant Beaver Brook, a place I love to canoe. En route to the put-in, I'd sometimes pass the water department, a concrete-floored garage that sheltered a few desks, a workshop, and a bunch of trucks. Once a year, the town hired divers, who pulled on disinfected wet suits and attacked the town's ninety-foot water tanks with vacuum cleaners. The system was simple and it worked well. At least until 1999, when tests revealed an outbreak of E. coli. Suddenly, Westford moved to the top of the list for federal Clean Water funding. Now, $14.2 million later, the town has two state-of-the-art treatment plants, complete with aeration towers, greensand filters, and an ultraviolet disinfection system.

The whole thing costs two million dollars a year to run. Is it really necessary? The source of the E. coli was never found, the department's superintendent tells me, and he heard of no one who'd gotten sick. In Breck Speed's world, people who live in towns where water treatment costs "too much" would revert to bottled water. His brand is cheap, he says, only $6.75 for five gallons. I do the math: to supply drinking (not cooking) water to a family of four would run upward of $200 a month. (That's the price today. As demand rises, clean water becomes scarce, and delivering it gets more expensive; Speed will probably raise his rates.)

Ditching tap water for bottled, the NRDC's Eric Goldstein says, "would be enormously expensive for society as a whole. It would leave vast quantities of Americans with the Hobson's choice of paying more for drinking water or relying on a public supply that could become increasingly inferior if it were abandoned by the elected officers and government decision makers."

It is tempting to think that the rise of bottled water reflects a simple shift from status consciousness to a concern with health and convenience. But to the pressure groups bent on running Nestlé out of small towns, and Coke off the face of the planet, drinking bottled water is a far more political act: it's an affirmation that water is a commodity, and that it's okay for corporations to control it.

The United Nations deems water a basic human right. But what does this mean? Sure, we all need water to live, but protecting and delivering it isn't free. Even in ancient Rome, where water came free to spigots built with public *scudi*, individuals paid extra to have water piped into their homes. Treating water as a commodity as well as a right is hardly a new idea. In fact, paying *more* for water in this country is probably the only way we're going to protect and improve it.

But who should do the protecting? Not private corporations, say Maude Barlow, of the Blue Planet Run Foundation, and Sara Ehrhardt, national water campaigner of the Council of Canadians. "The water we drink is simply too precious to trust to corporate hands, and too essential to rely on market forces alone to ensure equitable access and distribution," they write in *Grist* magazine. "The solution lies in declaring water as a human right and a public trust to be guarded by all levels of government; in sharing information and best practices on our public water systems; and in overseeing and protecting our public drinking water for future generations."

For antiprivatization groups, drinking bottled water when you've got safe tap water is traitorous. Gigi Kellett, associate campaigns director of Corporate Accountability International, links our obsession with Volvic and Voss to the looming privatization of public supplies, whether bottled or delivered through pipes, here or in the developing world. "We want to connect people here to the water crisis there, connect them to water protection in this country, and help them understand corporate control of water," she says. "To whom are we turning to provide water? Is it Coke, Nestlé, and Pepsi, or are we looking to locally controlled democratic cities and towns?"

I review my recent water-drinking history, struggling to make the argument concrete. Visiting a Midwestern college, I'm shocked to learn there's no drinking-water fountain in the gym. I row across New York Harbor with a group of college students, and while I sip from the public fountain near the shore, they hike ten minutes inland to buy Poland Spring at a store. Airports undergoing renovation keep losing their water fountains, while coolers stocked with Fiji proliferate. Well-maintained fountains are becoming about as scarce as working pay phones. At a rural New York State historic site, a bathroom sign warns visitors that an industrial contaminant has been found in the water. Just outside the bathroom: a Dasani-filled vending machine.

Cynically I think, "Why not?" If I were in the containerized-water business, I'd do everything in my power to either hide the bubblers or make public supplies look wildly unattractive. A new football stadium in Orlando, Florida, was built without a single water fountain; one hot afternoon, a dozen people were treated for heat exhaustion after the concession stands, which charged three bucks for a bottle of water, ran out. After the scandal hit the papers, fifty water fountains were quickly installed. At Lehigh University, in Pennsylvania, the dining-services company removed the free waterspouts from its Pepsi soda machines, steering students to bottled water. Only after much student protest did the spouts re-sprout.

It's easy for me to grok the domestic linkages between privatization and the loss of protection for our public supplies. But refusing Dasani in Des Plaines, I'm pretty sure, isn't going to help a thirsty Indian any more than cleaning your plate will help a starving African. Again, I ask Kellett to explain this connection. The first step, she says, are Corporate Accountability's taste tests: they're supposed to reveal that bottled water tastes no better than tap (don't try this in places with distinctive-tasting water). The second step is understanding that reliance on bottled water undermines confidence and investment in public water systems. And from there, it's on to India.

"Only by educating and mobilizing the public in the U.S.," Kellett says, can groups like hers "support international efforts to challenge corporate control and protect the fundamental human right to water." The logic of this argument remains vague to me, but the public criticism of the ecological impact of bottled water—its carbon footprint in particular—continues to gain traction: more and more local governments are canceling water contracts, and manufacturers of filters and reusable bottles are seeing record sales. Coke, Nestlé, and Fiji, among other bottlers, announced significant conservation efforts in 2007, though none scaled back on bottling. In fact, many operations expanded.

I admire the steps some companies have taken to shrink their carbon and water footprints, but I realize they will never satisfy antiprivatization groups until they quit profiting from water. Were clean water unlimited, of course, the issue of who owns it, and the morality of turning something so fundamental to life into a product controlled by private companies, wouldn't be nearly so crucial. But clean water *is* limited, and it's only getting more so.

Even before my first visit to Fryeburg, before my very first visit with Tom Brennan in the woods that buffered Poland Spring's source in Hollis, I had a vague idea that bottled water wasn't for me. It costs too much. Plus, I have no problem with tap. It tastes good to me, and in most places of the country it meets— or exceeds—federal and state standards.

But then I learned more about public water supplies—my own and that of other cities. Springwater, at that point, started to look pretty good. Unfortunately, I soon discovered, the companies that bottle springwater may sometimes threaten not only private wells and native ecosystems, but also native democracies. I considered, briefly, smaller-scale bottlers of fine waters from noble lineages. Michael Mascha, that day in Bryant Park, had been persuasive. But I couldn't stomach either their price or the road miles behind them. Surely there was something more sustainable, more local, out there.

How about purified tap? Aquafina and Dasani don't threaten swimming holes, springs, macro-invertebrates, native flora, or local control (at least in this country). They take their water from city supplies, delivered in preexisting pipes, sometimes gravity-fed. Robert Glennon, Mr. Let's Protect the Groundwater, who lives in Tucson, buys only purified tap. But Pepsi and Coke produce those waters, and I can't see giving my money to multinational corporations that take so much and leave so little behind (except trash). Nor are they bottling water in every city, let alone every state: gazillions of bottles are still being trucked across the country, at a high environmental cost.

The most responsible thing I can drink, I realize, is none of the above. It is something plentiful and superclean. It makes use of existing infrastructure, which is owned and operated by the people, is delivered by pipe instead of truck, and stresses neither aquifers nor the creatures that rely upon them. The answer, it seems, is reclaimed water. Or, in less euphemistic terms, toilet to tap.

NASA, which pays five grand to transport every kilogram of water into outer space, is all over the idea, with plans to outfit the International Space Station with a super-high-tech recycling system that purifies urine (and cooking and wash water and sweat) into pristine drinking water. Singapore overcame the yuck factor with NEWater, the stuff I'd sampled with Mascha. The Goreangab Reclamation Plant, in Windhoek, Namibia (the most arid of all the sub-Saharan countries), blends reservoir water with treated effluent to make up between 10 and 35 percent of the city's supply. Payson, Arizona, "recharges" its aquifer with treated sewage, which works its way through soil layers and eventually enters streams and then city reservoirs. The Upper Occoquan Sewage Authority, in Fairfax County, Virginia, has discharged recycled water to its reservoir for twenty-five years. Come to think of it, I was already getting a taste of toilet to tap: more than a hundred wastewater treatment plants discharge into New York City reservoirs. Our Department of Environmental Protection doesn't advertise the fact, but it's hardly a secret.

Tap-water drinkers in West Palm Beach haven't been so lucky, in terms of transparency. As reported in the *Palm Beach Post*, during a drought emergency in May of 2007, the city's utility briefly served its nearly 150,000 customers reclaimed sewage without even notifying them. Ordinarily, "reuse water"—which has been filtered, disinfected, and exposed to ultraviolet radiation—percolates through a grassy marsh for two years before it goes onto a well field, gets pumped into a canal that feeds reservoirs, and is piped into homes. In May, however, effluent was put directly onto the well field after being blended with water from old quarry pits. Because the city's drinking water met or exceeded federal standards, city officials decided there was no need to notify customers.

It could have been worse: for a brief, panicky moment engineers considered putting treated effluent directly into the water supply. The Florida Department of Health nixed the idea, reminding them that the water treatment plant wasn't equipped to remove sodium, nitrates, or chemical microconstituents such as hormones, antidepressants, or various "other unknowns." And then there were the psychological issues.

Residents of West Palm have come to accept recycled water only because—after all that filtering and percolating—it has lost its identity as sewage. Images of a grassy marsh are a big help: they transform something tainted by man into something found in nature. Brown becomes green becomes blue. Eliminate those intermediate steps, a spokesman from the department of environmental protection warned, "and public concern may surface."

The most important element in any toilet-to-tap scheme, of course, isn't stringent rules and rigorous enforcement but a massive public-relations campaign. Guided by the industry's best, officials in Orange County, California, held nine years' worth of pizza parties, water-treatment-plant tours, and public meetings to explain how sewer water could be purified and then added to underground water supplies for drinking. The $481 million project was inaugurated in November of 2007.

Just one day after the Santa Clara Valley water district, which serves San Jose, announced that it too would explore water reclamation, the district announced it would halt purchases of bottled water with public money. "We want to help educate the public that tap water is not only healthy and safe for them, but good for the environment," said the vice chair of the district's board. Communities in South Florida and Texas are also giving potable recycled wastewater serious consideration.

San Diego, which in the fall of 2007 tightened its already strict water-conservation measures, has been proposing and rejecting toilet-to-tap schemes for fifteen years. Among the more vocal opponents is a grassroots group called the Revolting Grandmas, who in their campaign against water reuse cite risks from endocrine disrupters, which end up in sewage when people either dump unused pharmaceuticals down the toilet or ingest and then excrete them.

There are good reasons to favor water reclamation (also called repurified water by those paid to promote it). It reduces pressure on freshwater supplies for nonpotable uses, such as watering golf courses and crops, and it enforces extreme cleanups of an end product that is otherwise dumped, significantly dirtier, into waterways that others drink from (or surf in, in the case of the Surfrider Foundation, part of the coalition that supports water recycling in San Diego). But reclamation systems are hugely expensive to build and run; they take many years to plan and construct; and some scientists doubt they can remove all pharmaceuticals and chemicals and neutralize the deadly 0157:H7. The National Research Council, in a 1998 report, concluded that reclaimed wastewater can be used to supplement drinking-water sources, but "only as a last resort and after a thorough health and safety evaluation." Dr. Steven Oppenheimer, director of the Center for Cancer and Developmental Biology at California State University, Northridge, likens drinking recycled water to playing Russian roulette with human life.

As bad as toilet-to-tap sounds, I have to remind myself: all water is recycled. The same droplets that misted early angiosperms and slaked the thirst of archaeopteryx are still around today. In nature, sunlight, soil, microbes, and the passage of time purify water. But when engineers inject sewage into aquifers, instead of letting it percolate slowly through the earth, soil scientist Frank Pecarich says, the process is short-circuited. "When you replace Mother Nature's system with tertiary treatment, you're leaving out the tremendous bacteria-cleansing mechanism of the soil it must go through before it reaches the aquifer. There has been great success in getting recycled water to flow through bogs, marshes, and particularly sand to get fairly clean water, in effect letting the whole world of biology go to work for you." But that's not the system being considered by many cities, and that's why Pecarich predicts toilet to tap will make people sick.

Honestly, the toilet-to-tap scenario—the one without massive dilution and a suitable lag between effluent and influent—

frightens me. There's too much room for human error: non-potable recycled drinking water has accidentally made it into drinking water in at least four cities within a decade. Recently, a cross-connection in Chula Vista, California, was found to have been delivering treated sewage to taps in a business park for two years. Then there are mechanical snafus (just pronouncing the words *membrane rupture* makes me shudder), and budget cuts, and system owners looking to turn a buck by looking the other way. Toilet to tap seems to be giving up, admitting we're out of options.

But that is hardly true. Water experts believe there is enough freshwater on the planet for everyone: it just isn't in the right place at the right time. So what can we do? Besides reclaiming polluted water with massive reverse osmosis machines, there are other so-called hard options, such as building storage dams and infrastructure to move water where we want it. We can desalinate water, but that's expensive and energy-intensive too.

Then there are the "soft" options, which emphasize efficiency (drip instead of flood irrigation) and better matching of water source to water use. For example, we can build new homes with "dual plumbing" that collects gray water (from sinks, showers, and washing machines) for such nonpotable uses as lawn watering or car washing. We can stop leaks: 14 percent of piped water disappears through holes and cracks. We can protect our water supplies by supporting legislators and advocacy groups that work to control polluters and to curb development in critical watersheds (see the appendix for a list of such organizations). We can revegetate urban areas, plant green roofs (which hold on to rainwater until it evaporates, instead of funneling it directly into storm drains), harvest rainwater in barrels and rain gardens, and restore wetlands along streams and rivers (marshes filter pesticides and nitrates, and some plants specialize in taking up heavy metals).

Inside our homes, we can practice good old-fashioned conservation. If all Americans cut their showers by one minute for a year, we'd conserve 161 billion gallons. Why does saving water matter if reservoirs are full? There are a couple of reasons. First, treating and delivering water takes energy: according to the EPA, letting a faucet run for five minutes consumes about as much energy as burning a sixty-watt incandescent lightbulb for fourteen hours. Second, once water runs down our pipes—in cities, that is—it isn't going to filter back through the earth into aquifers. It joins other waste streams from homes and businesses and storm drains, then gets pumped—much, much dirtier—into wastewater treatment plants. The more liquid that enters these facilities, the more energy and chemicals it takes to clean the water before it's discharged into the ocean or into a river that provides drinking water to another community downstream.

In homes with septic systems, excessive water use will overload the tank, causing it to fail—another reason to turn off taps while toothbrushing, to install low-flow toilets and showerheads, and to flush our toilets "selectively" (if it's yellow, let it mellow, et cetera). Conserving water, drought or no, leaves more behind for other living creatures up- and downstream, and it can help avoid the need to find or build new water sources and treatment plants. We may not need them today, but good habits take a while to form, and we will almost certainly need more water in the future.

Eating less meat isn't a bad idea either, in terms of water conservation: the water footprint of a four-ounce hamburger produced in California is 616 gallons. A cotton T-shirt is backed by 528.3 gallons of water, a single cup of coffee, 52.8. America uses more water per person than any other country in the Organization for Economic Cooperation and Development: about a hundred gallons a day. The British use thirty-one, and Ethiopians make do with just three.

Our leaders can more wisely allocate surface water and groundwater to their biggest users, farmers and industry. Does it make sense to grow water-intensive rice in the arid West? Can more industries use recycled water? Frito-Lay, for example, recently retooled its chip factory in Casa Grande, Arizona, to recycle 90 percent of its wastewater. Many utilities offer discounts to bulk users of water: raising rates inevitably leads to conservation.

Paying more to protect source water and upgrade infrastructure isn't impossible. Municipal water in this country is spectacularly underpriced—nationwide, about $2.50 for a thousand gallons. That consumers are willing to pay several thousand times more for bottled water that tastes good indicates we're willing to make some sacrifices for water that actually *is* good. Raising water rates is one answer; a tax on bottled water is another; and a clean-water trust fund, financed by industries that profit off of, or damage the quality of, clean water, is yet one more. ("We already have the money," a prominent environmental advocate tells me, "we've just decided to use it blowing up other countries' water infrastructure instead of fixing ours.")

When American Rivers and dozens of other watershed groups across the country polled a thousand voters on their attitudes about drinking water, a large majority wanted elected officials to take action to clean up polluted waters rather than have consumers adjust to problems by buying bottled water. It blows my mind that the groups even had to ask.

For now, what should we be drinking? The EPA tells us that the United States has one of the safest water supplies in the world. "I wouldn't hesitate to drink tap water anywhere in the country," Cynthia Dougherty, director of the EPA's Office of Groundwater and Drinking Water, says. Drink a glass of water in any city in the United States, Dr. Ronald B. Linsky of the National Water Research Institute said in "Avoiding Rate Shock: Making the Case for Water Rates," a report published by the American Water Works Association, and you "have a very, very high assurance of safe, high-quality drinking water." If you fall into no risk category, says the NRDC, you can drink most cities' tap water without a problem.

Statements like these confirm my personal bias: that water should be locally sourced, delivered by energy-efficient, publicly owned pipes, generate close to zero waste, and cost, for eight glasses a day, about forty-nine cents a year. Buy that water in bottles and you'd be spending $1,400.

But it isn't that simple: if it were, 20 percent of Americans wouldn't drink only bottled water. In 2006, 89.3 percent of the nation's nearly fifty-three thousand community water systems were in compliance with more than ninety EPA standards. That left 29.8 million people with water that missed the mark on either health or reporting standards, or both. (Many in this group live on Indian lands, and many drink from small systems, which have the most trouble meeting regulations.) Moreover, neither the EPA nor your water utility has anything to say about the condition of the pipes in your house. And then there are those risk categories.

"Right to know" reports advise the very young, the pregnant, the very old, or the immunocompromised (for example, people who are HIV-positive or undergoing chemotherapy) to consult with their doctors before drinking tap water, even in communities where water gets high marks. Some scientists define the at-risk population even more broadly, to include not just babies but children and teens, lactating women, and anyone over fifty-five. "Look at your annual report, then decide, based on your personal situation, if you need to do anything different," Dougherty says.

What's the big concern? It depends whom you ask; when you're a hammer, everything looks like a nail. Scientists who study lead worry about lead. Scientists who study the connection between chemicals and cancer worry about disinfection by-products. Microbiologists worry about tiny bugs.

Studies by epidemiologists indicate that at least seven million Americans experience gastrointestinal illnesses from waterborne microbes each year, of whom a thousand die. "Different people react to the same environment in different ways," says Ronnie D. Levin, a longtime EPA employee who is also a visiting scientist in the water and health program at the Harvard School of Public Health. "There is no bright golden line that says there's no risk." Seven million is too many, Levin says. "I did a cost-benefit analysis and I think we can do better than that, without increasing the amount of disinfectants in the water."

Levin is wary of using more chlorine and other disinfectants because they generate disinfection by-products, "none of which are good." Her solution? Require utilities that rely on surface water to filter it first, to remove organic contaminants, and then to disinfect, instead of the other way around.

Until those utilities retrofit, I ask Levin, what about bottled water?

There is uncertainty about that too, she says. "It really comes down to your comfort level. Bottled water's monitoring and enforcement aren't good." Because we don't know the results of plants' inspections, "it's a crapshoot what you're getting."

So what do you drink?

"You've got to go with what you've got." Tap, in other words.

Do you filter?

"I do the right thing," she says, which I take to mean yes.

By this point I've spoken to enough scientists and environmental experts to believe my countertop Brita is giving me more psychological than physical benefit, and that anyone with good reason to be suspicious of her tap water should invest in a point-of-use filter—the kind of gizmo you install on your faucet or under your sink. (Of pour-through filters, Levin says, "If there's nothing to filter out of your water, they are fine.") But not everyone is at high risk of illness, not everyone can afford a point-of-use filter and its maintenance (if they're not changed regularly, filters can put contaminants *into* water), and the money might better be spent on other preventive health measures.

To smooth out equity issues (under-the-sink filters can cost a couple hundred dollars to buy and plumb), Robert D. Morris, the epidemiologist, suggests that utilities help pay for, install, and maintain point-of-use devices. In that way, water utilities could have confidence, he writes in *The Blue Death*, "that occasional occurrences of accidental, incidental, or intentional contamination would have little if any consequence." What would that cost? I ask him. "About a third of the utility's annual cost," he says, "but it's onetime only. You'd amortize that cost, and you'd recycle the filters. There are economies of scale in buying a lot of them. But, yes, the consumer will ultimately pay for it."

All these caveats beg the question: how do I know if I should be suspicious of my water? The EPA says, "Read your annual water report." But these documents—written by the utility—can be flawed, and some are essentially propaganda. (And again, they say nothing about the condition of your pipes.) They report yearly averages over time and, with some contaminants, over multiple locations within a system, which can obscure spikes. They don't necessarily list contaminants that aren't regulated (such as perchlorate, radon, and MTBE), and their reporting periods close long before data reach customers. Reports may state that finished water has no cryptosporidium, but the protozoan parasite is notoriously difficult to detect.

When the NRDC studied the water-quality reports of nineteen cities in 2001, it gave five of them a poor or failing grade for burying, obscuring, and omitting findings about health effects of contaminants in city water supplies, printing misleading statements, and violating a number of right-to-know requirements, such as the rule that says reports must identify known sources of pollutants in city water. What's a devotee of the tap to do? Read your report carefully, learn about the health effects of contaminants, call your utility with questions, then test your water yourself (see the appendix for sources to help you with all of this).

Drinking the waters of the Ashokan and other upstate reservoirs, here in New York City, my husband and I fall into no obvious risk category, but could eight-year-old Lucy fight off cryptosporidiosis? (Treatment with ultraviolet light hasn't yet started.) And while disinfection by-products worry me a little (I live far from where the chlorine goes in, which gives trihalomethanes a longer time to build up), do they worry me enough to spend another hundred bucks a year on filters?

To settle the question, I order my own tests. I fill four different containers with unfiltered tap water and mail them on ice to a certified lab in Ypsilanti, Michigan. When I rip open the envelope in two weeks, I'm relieved: I've got no lead, no coliform, no nitrates, and my total trihalomethanes are well within federal limits (at least on this November day: they may be higher in the heat of summer). But my manganese—of all things—is 40 percent higher than the federal standard (though still 5.7 times lower than that tasty Gerolsteiner I drank in Bryant Park). My Brita won't remove the mineral, but according to experts, this level presents no health risk to either children or adults. Steven Schindler, my water-testing guru at the Department of Environmental Protection, says the city never exceeded the state's limit of 0.3 parts per million in 2007. (The federal limit is 0.05 parts per million, but it's a "secondary level," which means utilities aren't required to test for it; the contaminant affects only the aesthetics of the water. At long last, the mystery of the reddish fuzz in the bottom of my Brita appears to be solved.) If manganese is my only problem, I'm happy. Like the vast majority of Americans, I can keep drinking tap water without worry.

I come away from my investigations with at least one certainty: not all tap water is perfect. But it is the devil we know, the devil we have standing to negotiate with and to improve. Bottled-water companies don't answer to the public, they answer to shareholders. As Alan Snitow and Deborah Kaufman write in *Thirst*, "If citizens no longer control their most basic resource, their water, do they really control anything at all?"

Bottled water does have its place—it's useful in emergencies and essential for people whose health can't tolerate even filtered water. But it's often no better than tap water, its environmental and social price is high, and it lets our public guardians off the hook for protecting watersheds, stopping polluters, upgrading treatment and distribution infrastructure, and strengthening treatment standards.

Certainly, nearly everything humans do has an environmental impact—biking to work, recycling newspapers, and drinking tap water included. But understanding that impact is the first step toward reducing it. It's true that the impact of bottled water looks minuscule next to other water uses—growing beef, say, or manufacturing cars. But try telling that to someone who lives on a springwater truck route or who drinks from a well that shares an aquifer with a commercial pump. As Lucy sings out when I try to tell her that some problem of hers is trivial in the larger scheme of things, "Not for me-eeee."

If someday I find myself wanting to buy bottled water, I will do it as an informed consumer, someone who knows that the images on the label may not reflect an ecological reality, that part of its sticker price may be landing in the pockets of lawyers and PR flacks, that profits probably aren't benefiting those who live near the source, and that the bottle and its transportation have a significant carbon footprint. And then I will try to drink with the fullest pleasure; pleasure that, to quote Wendell Berry on the pleasure of eating, "does not depend on ignorance."

I started my water investigations in Fryeburg, Maine, where Howard Dearborn insists Poland Spring is ruining his pond. Is it? Possibly, because pumping leaves less water to dilute phosphorus, which seem to be spurring excessive plant growth. Does the pumping affect other ecosystems? Unclear—but the argument that there's no such thing as "excess" water is compelling: all that Poland Spring water—180 million gallons a year—used to reach downstream ecosystems before it was diverted to tanker trucks. Are the trucks annoying, and potentially dangerous? Yes. Does the town get any benefit from the operation? It did, a bit, when income from Pure Mountain Springs kept rates down. But after the buyout, who knows what will happen? If Poland Spring builds a bottling plant, some will get jobs, but the town, as a whole, may suffer.

And then there's an even more important question: is it right—forget about legal, for a moment—for an outside corporation to contradict the wishes of the community? Increasingly, citizens are thinking not. In tiny towns across the nation, grassroots groups, connected by the Internet and cheered on by antiglobalization activists, are fighting such intrusions—from confined-animal-feeding operations in Iowa, to landfills in rural Pennsylvania, to Wal-Marts in suburbs everywhere. By organizing and educating themselves, the activists of Fryeburg—intentionally or not—have joined this citizens' movement.

As consumers turn away from failing water systems, as good water becomes scarce, and as private companies dig ever more boreholes, squabbling over water will intensify. Fryeburg doesn't look anything like Cochabamba, Bolivia, where massive street demonstrations erupted in 2000 after a Bechtel subsidiary privatized the water system; or Kerala, India, where villages continue to fight with Coca-Cola over groundwater allocation; or even Groveland, Florida, which is both facing water shortages and entertaining offers from a California-based company to pump and bottle 182 million gallons of groundwater a year—a third of what the town currently consumes. But in asking who owns water and attempting to keep private interests from taking and selling it for outsize profits, Fryeburg is a microcosm of the worldwide frenzy to control this precious resource.

On a late-summer morning, a couple of months after the Supreme Judicial Court remanded the tanker decision to the planning board, I slid a kayak down a steep, wooded bank and into the Saco River. On this overcast day, only a few canoeists were paddling through the several miles of curves that slice through floodplain forest to Walker's Bridge, and it was quiet for long stretches of time. The water was just as I remembered it from childhood camping trips: gin clear. Century-old silver maples— some with rope swings—canted over undercut banks. On the outside curves, where the current had formed wide sandy beaches, it was easy to pull out and swim. Drifting along, I was transfixed by the sinuous striations on the river bottom—golden here, purplish black there. I knew by then why the water was so clear, and I knew why Poland Spring coveted it. I knew that when the river overflowed in the spring, it enriched the soil and nurtured rare plants, it fed the farms, and it sustained the soul of Fryeburg.

Thousands of years ago, the Wabanaki Indians paddled this same stretch. Would Lucy, when she grows up, bring her children to swim in the Saco, to delight in its clear water and sandy bottom? There is no guarantee. It's easy to ask what one or two boreholes in the Wards Brook aquifer can do. But it isn't just Poland Spring pumping: the town has its well, there's a well behind the Dearborn Precision Tubular Products plant (so far, not in use), and the WE Corporation has one too. Every gallon of water that thunders into a tanker truck represents a measure that doesn't seep through the aquifer and into wetlands, another gallon that isn't diluting the pollutants that run into the Saco from roads, farms, septic tanks, and industry.

If Poland Spring succeeds in building a bottling plant in Fryeburg, the company will need another source of water to feed it, in addition to the Wards Brook gallons: the town is full of landowners with springs. Who knows what will happen next? Or what will happen upstream? A New Hampshire water company recently announced plans to drill new wells in the Saco River floodplain, just over the state line from Fryeburg, to water a housing development. The deal screeched to a halt after local officials, who'd been warily eyeing Fryeburg's trials, discovered the company planned to pump five times more than the development required.

Several months after my paddle, I talk to Scott Gamwell, who helped organize the fight against the tanker station in East Fryeburg and is now scrambling to raise money for his group's ongoing legal fees. If Poland Spring stays in town, he says, it might be all right for it to take just 5 percent of the "excess" water in the Wards Brook aquifer, instead of the current 75.

"Do you think that amount of water would make it worthwhile for the company?" I ask.

"Not today," he says, "but in 2030, it might."

ACKNOWLEDGMENTS

Many people generously helped me report this book—some of their names appear in the text. I'd like to offer special thanks, in Fryeburg, to Jim Wilfong, Stefan Jackson, and Howard Dearborn, who, despite threatening to throw me in the lake, welcomed me back to Lovewell Pond. Tom Brennan, of Nestlé Waters North America, was patient with my questions and unstinting with his time, as was Mike Klender in Kansas City, Jennifer Sass at the Natural Resources Defense Council, and Emily Lloyd and Steven Schindler in New York City. Thanks to Lisa Reed for the NEWater, to Leigh Baker for research assistance, and to Joshua Royte for fine lodgings and botanical guidance.

There have been several books written about the global water crisis, all of them increasingly important as we diminish this most precious of natural resources, and I'm grateful to have had the benefit of those authors' experiences (see Selected Bibliography and Further Reading). Special thanks to the Overbrook Foundation—which supports many remarkably effective conservation projects and whose financial support made researching and writing this book in a short time possible and at times even pleasant—and to Daniel Katz, who was particularly enthusiastic.

A tip of the hat to Jonathan Gregg at the Vermont Studio Center for his timely intervention. Portions of this book appeared in altered form in *Grist* magazine, thanks to Tom Philpott, and in the *New York Times*, thanks to Frank Flaherty.

For helping me navigate among many twisting channels of reporting, I'm indebted to my editor, Gillian Blake, who held up green lights and red lights as needed. Finally, this book wouldn't exist without the advice and encouragement of my husband, Peter Kreutzer, who, in addition to editorial heavy lifting, suffered my lamentations, cooked nonstop delectable meals, and wrangled Lucy, my ultimate audience and inspiration.

APPENDIX

Below is a list of Internet sources for more information on the topics covered in this book, as well as information on how to learn more about water quality in your area.

General information from the Environmental Protection Agency (EPA) on tap water:
www.epa.gov/safewater and http://www.epa.gov/OGWDW/faq/faq .html

The Environmental Working Group on contaminants in tap water:
http://www.ewg.org/tapwater/findings.php

The Natural Resources Defense Council (NRDC) on contaminants in tap water:
http://www.nrdc.org/water/drinking/fdrinkingwater.pdf

The EPA on testing for contaminants in well water:
http://www.epa.gov/safewater/privatewells/index2.html

An NRDC report on tap-water quality and compliance:
http://www.nrdc.org/water/drinking/uscities/pdf/chap02.pdf

The U.S. Geological Survey on "emerging contaminants" in drinking water:
http://toxics.usgs.gov/regional/emc/index.html

Information from the Consumer Federation of America on contaminants of concern for vulnerable populations:
http://www.consumerfed.org/pdfs/vulnpop.pdf

The Centers for Disease Control and Prevention on preventing cryptosporidiosis in vulnerable populations:
http://www.cdc.gov/ncidod/dpd/parasites/cryptosporidiosis/factsht_crypto_prevent_ci.htm

The Campaign for Safe and Affordable Drinking Water's "Making Sense of 'Right to Know' Reports":
http://www.safe-drinking-water.org/pdf/makesense.pdf

The Department of Health and Human Services on the health effects of possible water contaminants:
www.atsdr.cdc.gov/toxpro2.html

To find a state-certified lab to test your water, see:
http://www.epa.gov/safewater/labs/index.html or call the Safe Drinking Water Hotline, 800-426-4791. For more information on when or what to test for, see http://www.epa.gov/safewater/faq/pdfs/fs_homewatertesting.pdf.

Physicians for Social Responsibility fact sheets on safe drinking water:
http://www.psr.org/site/PageServer?pagename=Safe_Drinking_Water_main

On tap-water filters:
From Food and Water Watch:
http://www.foodandwaterwatch.org/water/know-your-water/home-water-filters/tap-water-filtration-guide
From *Grist* magazine:
http://www.grist.org/advice/possessions/2004/05/04/mcrandle-bottled/index.html

From *Consumer Reports* (May 2007), a primer on water-filter types:
http://www.consumerreports.org/cro/home-garden/kitchen/water-filters/water-filters-5-07/types/0507_filter_types.htm (recommendations and ratings available by subscription only)

FDA definitions of different types of bottled water:
http://www.cfsan.fda.gov/~acrobat/botwatr.pdf

How to purify water in an emergency:
http://www.wikihow.com/Purify-Water

Fluoride in your tap water?
In favor: http://www.cdc.gov/fluoridation/
Opposed: http://www.fluoridealert.org

To learn more about water and privatization:
The Alliance for Democracy: http://www.thealliancefordemocracy.org/water/
Blue Planet Project: www.blueplanetproject.net
Corporate Accountability International: www.stopcorporateabuse.org
Defending Water in Maine: www.defendingwaterinmaine.org
Food and Watch Watch: http://www.thealliancefordemocracy.org/water/
H_2O for ME: http://www.h2oforme.com
McCloud Watershed Council: http://mccloudwatershedcouncil.org
Michigan Citizens for Water Conservation: http://www.savemiwater.org
The Pacific Institute for Studies in Development, Environment and Security: http://www.pacinst.org
The Polaris Institute: www.polarisinstitute.org
Save Our Groundwater: www.saveourgroundwater.org
The Sierra Club's Water Privatization Taskforce: http://www.sierraclub.org/committees/cac/water/
Sweetwater Alliance: http://www.waterissweet.org
Water Dividend Trust: http://www.waterdividendtrust.com
Water Waves: http://waterwaves.org/Site/Welcome.html

Organizations working to protect public waterways:
American Rivers: www.americanrivers.org

American Whitewater: www.americanwhitewater.org
Clean Water Action: www.cleanwateraction.org
Clean Water Network: http://www.cleanwaternetwork.org
Clearwater Hudson River Sloop: www.clearwater.org
Conservation International: www.conservation.org
Earth Justice: www.earthjustice.org/our_work/issues/water/
Earth Policy Institute: www.earth-policy.org
Environmental Defense: www.environmentaldefense.org
The Freshwater Society: www.freshwater.org
League of Conservation Voters: www.lcv.org
The Nature Conservancy: www.nature.org/initiatives/freshwater/
The River Network: www.rivernetwork.org
Trout Unlimited: www.tu.org
Waterkeeper Alliance: www.waterkeeper.org
World Wildlife Fund: www.panda.org

Other organizations:
American Waterworks Association: www.awwa.org
Association of Metropolitan Water Agencies: www.amwa.net
International Bottled Water Association: www.bottledwater.org
Water Environment Federation: http://wef.org/Home

SELECTED BIBLIOGRAPHY AND FURTHER READING

(Books, articles, and reports I used to research this book)

Adams, Glen. "Bill sets new rules for water extraction." *Kennebec Journal*, June 22, 2007.

Alexander, Jeff. "Bottler aims to take more from rivers." *Muskegon Chronicle*, December 3, 2005.

"Analysis of the February, 1999 Natural Resources Defense Council Report on Bottled Water." Drinking Water Research Foundation, 1999.http://www.dwrf.info/nrdc_bottled_water.htm#executive%20summary.

Andronaco, Meg. "Bottled water is healthy for people and the environment." *Tallahassee Democrat*, March 8, 2007.

Arnold, Emily, and Janet Larsen. "Bottled water: Pouring resources down the drain." Earth Policy Institute, February 2, 2006. http://www.earth-policy.org/Updates/2006/Update51.htm.

Baerren, Eric. "Proposal says a lot about water quality." *Mt. Pleasant (MI) Morning Sun*, November 24, 2006.

———. *Blue Covenant: The Global Water Crisis and the Coming Battle for the Right to Water.* New York: New Press, 2008.

Barlow, Maude, and Tony Clarke. *Blue Gold: The Fight to Stop the Corporate Theft of the World's Water.* New York: New Press, 2003.

Barnes, Diane, and Jack Barnes. *Pictorial History of Fryeburg: Upper Saco River Valley: Fryeburg, Lovell, Brownfield, Denmark, and Hiram.* Portsmouth, NH: Arcadia Publishing, 2002.

Barnett, Cynthia. *Mirage: Florida and the Vanishing Water of the Eastern U.S.* Ann Arbor: University of Michigan Press, 2007.

Barrett, Joe. "How ethanol is making the farm belt thirsty." *Wall Street Journal,* September 5, 2007.

Beckhardt, Jon. "Considering Chloramine." *San Francisco Bay Guardian,* June 13, 2007.

Blanding, Michael. "The Bottled Water Lie." *AlterNet,* October 26, 2006. www.alternet.org/story/43480.

Branch, Shelly. "Waiters reveal tricks of the trade to raise the bottled-water pressure." *Wall Street Journal,* March 8, 2002.

Carkhuff, David. "Real money from Fryeburg water made by reseller to Poland Spring." *Conway Daily Sun,* December 21, 2004.

———. "Report: Fryeburg aquifer already stretched too thin." *Conway Daily Sun,* September 8, 2005.

———. "Rare turtle muddies waters of Poland Spring filling station." *Conway Daily Sun,* November 9, 2005.

Chapelle, Frank. *Wellsprings: A Natural History of Bottled Spring Waters.* Piscataway, NJ: Rutgers University Press, 2005.

Christen, Kris. "Removing emerging contaminants from drinking water." *Environmental Science and Technology,* November 21, 2007.

Clairmonte, Frederick, and John Cavanagh. *Merchants of Drink: Transitional Control of World Beverages.* Washington, DC: Institute for Policy Studies, 1994.

Clarke, Tony. *Inside the Bottle: An Exposé of the Bottled Water Industry.* Ottawa, ON: Polaris Institute, 2007.

Clayworth, Jason. "Ethanol stirs fear of water shortage." *Des Moines Register,* July 19, 2007.

"Clean water is a right: but it also needs to have a price." *Economist,* November 9, 2006.

"Clear choices for clean drinking water." *Consumer Reports,* January 2003.

Cone, Marla. "Public health agency linked to chemical industry." *Los Angeles Times,* March 4, 2007.

Cromwell, John E., Joel B. Smith, and Robert S. Raucher. "Implications of Climate Change for Urban Water Utilities." Washington, DC: Association of Metropolitan Water Agencies, December 2007.

Deutsch, Claudia H. "For Fiji Water, a Big List of Green Goals." *New York Times,* November 7, 2007.

———. "Two growing markets that start at your tap." *New York Times*, November 10, 2007.

De Villiers, Marc. *Water: The Fate of Our Most Precious Resource.* Boston: Mariner Books, 2001.

Fahrenthold, David A. "Bottlers, states and the public slug it out in water war." *Washington Post,* June 12, 2006.

Ferrier, Catherine. "Bottled water: Understanding a social phenomenon." World Wildlife Fund, April 2001. http://www.panda.org/livingwaters/pubs/bottled_water.pdf.

Fishman, Charles. "Message in a bottle." *Fast Company,* July 2007.

Galusha, Diane. *Liquid Assets: A History of New York City's Water System.* Fleischmanns, NY: Harbor Hill Books, 2002.

Gentile, Beth-Ann F. "Groundwater in Maine: A time for action." Fryeburg, ME: H2O for ME, September 2006.

Gertner, Jon. "The future is drying up." *New York Times Magazine,* October 21, 2007.

Gitlitz, Jennifer, and Pat Franklin. "Water, Water Everywhere: The Growth of Non-Carbonated Beverages in the United States." Container Recycling Institute, February 2007. http://container-recycling.org/assets/pdfs/reports/2007-waterwater.pdf.

Glausiusz, Josie. "Toxic salad: What are fecal bacteria doing on our leafy greens?" *Discover,* April 2007.

Gleick, Peter H., et al. *The World's Water 2006–2007: The Biennial Report on Freshwater Resources.* Washington, DC: Island Press, 2006.

Glennon, Robert. *Water Follies: Groundwater Pumping and the Fate of America's Fresh Waters.* Washington, DC: Island Press, 2004.

———. "Water Scarcity, Marketing, and Privatization." *Texas Law Review* 83, no 7 (June 2005).

Grossman, Elizabeth. "Chemicals May Play Role in Rise in Obesity." *Washington Post,* March 12, 2007.

Gunther, Marc. "Bottled water: No longer cool?" *Fortune,* April 2007.

Harkness, Seth. "Few laws guard water." *Portland Press Herald,* December 19, 2005.

———. "Legal fight erodes appeal of Poland Spring's plan for bottling plant." *Portland Press Herald,* November 26, 2007.

Howard, Brian C. "Despite the hype, bottled water is neither cleaner nor greener than tap water." *E/The Environmental Magazine,* September–October, 2003.

"It's only water, right?" *Consumer Reports*, August 2000.

Jamison, Michael. "Testing reveals drugs' residue." *Missoulian*, June 28, 2007.

Khamsi, Roxanne. "Plastics chemical harms eggs in unborn mice." *New Scientist*, January 12, 2007.

Koeppel, Gerard T. *Water for Gotham: A History*. Princeton, NJ: Princeton University Press, 2001.

Kummer, Corby. "Carried away." *New York Times Magazine*, August 30, 1998.

Langeveld, M. Dirk. "Decision a setback for water-facility plan." *Lewiston (ME) Sun Journal*, November 15, 2007.

Lavelle, Marianne. "Water woes." *U.S. News & World Report*, June 4, 2007.

Levin, Ronnie, Paul R. Epstein, Tim E. Ford, Winston Harrington, Erik Olson, and Eric G. Reichard. "U.S. drinking water challenges in the 21st century." *Environmental Health Perspectives* 110, no. S1 (February 2002).

Martin, Andrew. "In eco-friendly factory, low-guilt potato chips." *New York Times*, November 15, 2007.

Martin, Glen. "Bottled water war heats up election: Pitched battle to control board as former timber town weighs Nestlé's McCloud River plan." *San Francisco Chronicle*, November 5, 2006.

Marx, Robin, and Eric A. Goldstein. *A Guide to New York City's Reservoirs and Their Watersheds*. New York: Natural Resources Defense Council, 1993.

Mascha, Michael. *Fine Waters: A Connoisseur's Guide to the World's Most Distinctive Bottled Waters*. Philadelphia: Quirk Books, 2006.

Meeker-Lowry, Susan. "Earth Notes: Be careful with 'our' water." *Bridgton (ME) News*, August 25, 2005.

Midkiff, Ken. *Not a Drop to Drink: America's Water Crisis (And What You Can Do)*. Novato, CA: New World Library, 2007.

Miller, Kevin. "H2O takes new tack against big bottlers." *Bangor (ME) Daily News*, March 2, 2007.

Morris, Robert D. *The Blue Death: Disease, Disaster, and the Water We Drink*. New York: HarperCollins, 2007.

———. "Pipe Dreams." *New York Times*, October 3, 2007.

Moskin, Julia. "Must be something in the water." *New York Times*, February 15, 2006.

"A National Assessment of Tap Water Quality." Environmental Working Group, December 20, 2005. www.ewg.org/tapwater.

Normandeau Associates. "Baseline Characterization of Natural Resources of Wards Brook and Lovewell Pond in Support of Assessment of Potential Groundwater Withdrawal Impacts." Bedford, NH: November 2007.

Olsen, Erik D. "Bottled Water: Pure Drink or Pure Hype?" Washington, DC: Natural Resources Defense Council, February 1999. http://www.nrdc.org/water/drinking/bw/bwinx.asp.

Pearce, Fred. *When the Rivers Run Dry: Water—the Defining Crisis of the Twenty-first Century.* Boston: Beacon Press, 2006.

Pecarich, Frank. "Irrigating your vegetables with treated sewage water? Still not a good idea if you are concerned about E. coli." *California Progress Report,* January 5, 2007. http://www.californiaprogressreport.com/2007/01/irrigating_your.html.

Pibel, Doug. "Communities take power." *Yes!* magazine, Fall 2007.

Postel, Sandra. *Last Oasis: Facing Water Scarcity.* New York: Norton, 1997.

Reisner, Marc. *Cadillac Desert: The American West and Its Disappearing Water.* New York: Penguin, 1993.

Shaw, Bob. "New 3M chemical find prompts state to offer bottled water to six homes." *Pioneer Press,* June 27, 2007.

Sheehan, Viola. *The Saco River: A History and Canoeing Guide.* Saco, ME: The Saco River Corridor Association, 1976.

Shiva, Vandana. *Water Wars: Privatization, Pollution and Profit.* Cambridge, MA: South End Press, 2002.

Singer, Stacey. "WPB water supply got boost from treated sewage." *Palm Beach Post,* June 17, 2007.

Snitow, Alan, Deborah Kaufman, and Michael Fox. *Thirst: Fighting the Corporate Theft of Our Water.* San Francisco: Jossey-Bass, 2007.

Speed, Breck. "Is tap 'just as good' as bottled water?" Press release, August 23, 2007.

Spencer, Theo. "Something to gush about." *Gourmet,* February 2000.

Spivak, Jeffrey. "The big muddy: Plenty of drops to drink." *Kansas City Star,* June 28, 2006.

"Trouble Downstream: Upgrading Conservation Compliance." Environmental Working Group, September 4, 2007. http://www.ewg.org/reports/compliance.

Turkel, Tux. "Water deal too sweet?" *Portland Press Herald,* April 1, 2007.

————. "Consumption of bottled water soars." *Portland Press Herald*, August 12, 2007.

Wilfong, Jim. "Who owns Maine's water: Nestlé or the people?" *On the Commons*. www.OntheCommons.org/node/1118.

Wright, Virginia. "Troubled waters" *Down East* magazine, May 2006.

————. "Water power." *Bates* magazine, Fall 2006.

Yardley, William. "Gaping reminders in cities of aging, crumbling pipes." *New York Times*, February 8, 2007.

INDEX

1/11 (8) 12/09

12/12 (8) 12/09

1/15 (9) 5/14